RAMEN FOR BEGINNERS

1000 Days of Healthy Delicious Easy Ramen Recipes to Enjoy and Make Both Traditional and Vibrant New Ramen in the Comfort of Your Home| Full Color Version

SAYA TSUDA

Copyright© 2023 By Saya Tsuda Rights Reserved

This book is copyright protected. It is only for personal use. You cannot amend, distribute, sell, use, quote or paraphrase any part of the content within this book, without the consent of the author or publisher.

Under no circumstances will any blame or legal responsibility be held against the publisher, or author, for any damages, reparation, or monetary loss due to the information contained within this book, either directly or indirectly.

Disclaimer Notice:

Please note the information contained within this document is for educational and entertainment purposes only. All effort has been executed to present accurate, up to date, reliable, complete information. No warranties of any kind are declared or implied. Readers acknowledge that the author is not engaged in the rendering of legal, financial, medical or professional advice. The content within this book has been derived from various sources. Please consult a licensed professional before attempting any techniques outlined in this book.

By reading this document, the reader agrees that under no circumstances is the author responsible for any losses, direct or indirect, that are incurred as a result of the use of the information contained within this document, including, but not limited to, errors, omissions, or inaccuracies.

Table of Contents

Introduction	1
Chapter 1	
Basics of Ramen	2
History of Ramen	3
Essential Ingredients for Making a Bowl of Ramen	4
Essential Tools	5
Optional Tools	6
Chapter 2	
Broth & Tare	7
Basic Clear Chicken Soup	8
Traditional Clear Chicken Soup	8
Tonkotsu Creamy Soup	9
Basic Chicken Broth	9
Mushroom Broth	9
Basic Pork Broth	10
Basic Fish Broth	10
Shio Tare	10
Basic Vegan Broth (Kombu Dashi)	11
Easy-and-Quick Clear Soup	11
Miso Tare	11
Kare (Curry) Coconut Tare	12
Basic Beef Broth	12
Shoyu Tare	13
Thick Vegetarian Creamy Soup	13
Spicy Miso Tare	13

Chapter 3	
Toppings	14
Pork Chashu	15
Chicken Chashu	15
Niku Soboro (Minced Meat Topping)	16
Negi (Scallion) Oil	16
Seasoned Bamboo Shoots	16
Roasted Tomatoes	17
Ajitama Eggs	17
Marinated Bean Sprouts	18
La-Yu Chili Oil	18
Mayu (Black Garlic Paste)	19
Ginger Pork	19
Chicken Karaage	20
Teriyaki Pork Tenderloin	20
Soy Sauce Eggs	21
Shio Kakuni Pork	21
Menma	22
Pickled Daikon Radish	22
Roasted Kabocha Squash	23
Tamagoyaki (Japanese Omelet)	23
Ebi Abura (Shrimp Oil)	24
Sesame Paste	24
Chapter 4	
Shio Ramen	25
Basic Shio Ramen	26
Traditional Shio Ramen	26

Green Vegetable Shio Ramen	27
Shio Ramen with Corn, Roasted Tomatoes, and Basil	27
Shio Ramen with Ginger Chicken and Bok Choy	28
Shio Ramen with Crispy Pork Belly, Scallions, Seasoned Bamboo Shoots, and Nori	28
Shio Ramen with Ham and Shiitake Mushrooms	29
Shio Ramen with Buttery Clams	29
Shio Ramen with Shredded Pork and Sesame-Chili Oil	30
Shio Ramen with 5-Spice Beef Short Ribs	30
Scallion-Flavored Shio Ramen	31
Shio Ramen with Curried Beef with Peas and Carrots	31
Vegan Kare Shio	32
Shiitake Shio Ramen with Crab, Corn, and Pickled Daikon Radish	32
Shio Ramen with Chashu Pork Belly, Clams and Black Truffle Oil	33
Shio Ramen with Crispy Fried Squid, Squid Ink, and Salmon Roe	33
Hakodate Shio Ramen with Spicy Ground Chicken	33
Shio Ramen with Ginger Chicken, Soy Sauce Eggs, and Yuzu	34
Shiitake Shio Ramen with Silken Tofu, Mushrooms, and Crispy Shallots	34
Teriyaki Chicken and Salmon Shio	35
Spring Shio Ramen with Baby Bok Choy, Peas, and Soft-Boiled Eggs	35

Chapter 5
Shoyu Ramen — 36

Traditional Shoyu Ramen	37
Vegan Shoyu Ramen	37
Shoyu Ramen with Panko-Breaded Chicken and Spinach	37
Shoyu Ramen with Sake-Steamed Chicken Drumsticks	38
Shoyu Ramen with Crispy Chicken Strips	38
Shoyu Ramen with Bacon, Soft-Boiled Eggs, and Crispy Kale	39
Shoyu Chicken Ramen with Miso-Glazed Carrots	39
Shoyu Ramen with Panfried Shrimp and Greens	40
Shoyu Ramen with Pork Katsu, Spinach, and Chili Oil	40
Shoyu Ramen with Lemony Breaded Halibut	41
Kitakata Ramen	41
Onomichi Ramen	42
Shoyu Ramen with Crispy Shredded Pork and Arugula	42
Shoyu Shrimp Tempura Ramen	43
Shoyu Ramen with Ginger-Braised Pork and Kimchi	43
Shoyu Ramen with Seared Steak, Scallions, and Sesame Oil	44
Shoyu Ramen with Chicken Katsu, Broccoli Rabe, and Scallions	44
Halal Shoyu Ramen	45
Black-Garlic Shoyu Ramen	45

Chapter 6
Miso Ramen — 46

Traditional Miso Ramen	47
Wakame (Seaweed) Miso Ramen	47
Miso Ramen with Braised Chicken Thighs	47
Miso Ramen with Garlic Chicken and Soy Sauce Eggs	48
Miso-Ginger Ramen with Chicken and Blackened Lemons	48
Miso Ramen with Crispy Pork Katsu and Black Garlic Oil	48
Miso Curry Soy Milk Ramen	48
Peanut Miso	49
Spicy Miso Ramen with Grilled Pork Tenderloin	49
Sapporo Seafood Miso	49
Spicy Miso Ramen with Crispy Fried Chicken	50
Miso Pumpkin Ramen with Pan-Fried Tofu and Bok Choy	50
Creamy Miso Chicken Ramen with Chashu Pork Belly and Maitake Mushrooms	50

Chapter 7
Tonkotsu Ramen — 51

Traditional Tonkotsu Ramen	52
Negi-Baka Tonkotsu Ramen	52
Hakata Ramen	52
Shoyu Tonkotsu with Shrimp and Mushrooms	53
Wakayama Ramen	53
Classic Tonkotsu Ramen with Chashu Pork and Soy Sauce Eggs	53
Hakata-Style Mountain Of Scallions Ramen	54
Tonkotsu Shio Ramen	54
Spicy Tonkotsu Ramen with Grilled Pork Tenderloin, Peanuts, and Cilantro	54
Creamy Tonkotsu Ramen	55
Mayu Tonkotsu Ramen	55
Spicy Miso Tonkotsu Ramen with Ginger Pork	55

Chapter 8
Other Ramen — 56

Hiyashi Chuka (Cold Chinese-Style Noodles)	57
Vegan Hiyashi Chuka (Cold Chinese Noodles)	57
Morioka-Style Cold Ramen	57
Yakisoba-Style Ramen with Garlic, Chili, and Sesame Oil	57
Yamagata Cold Ramen	58
Tantanmen	58
Laksa-Style Ramen with Soft-Boiled Eggs, Green Beans, and Bean Sprouts	58
Tsukemen	59
Tokyo-Style Tsukemen	59
Pork Ramen with Kimchi, Fried Eggs, and Spam	59
Salt-Broiled Salmon Ramen with Corn and Greens	60
Tantanmen with Spicy Sesame Pork	60
Vegetarian Curry Ramen with Carrots, Peas, and Soft-Boiled Eggs	60
Thai-Style Green Curry Ramen with Grilled Steak, Squash, and Greens	61
Vegan Chili Tofu Ramen	61

Appendix 1 Measurement Conversion Chart — 62
Appendix 2 The Dirty Dozen and Clean Fifteen — 63
Appendix 3 Index — 64

Introduction

Nearly everyone knows about ramen. It is a must-try food when someone goes to Japan. Japanese culture is both old and rich. Ramen was introduced to the world by Japan. However, ramen is not bound to any culture. Chinese travelers introduced chicken broth to the Japanese people in the 1850s.

Japanese people modified it, and now it's called ramen. It is a kind of soupy noodle with vegetables, egg, meat, pork, and many other ingredients. At that time, blue-collar workers liked eating ramen because it was quick, tasty, and budget-friendly. And now, it is an unavoidable part of Japanese cuisine.

I grew up loving ramen. It was the only thing I could eat daily. Unfortunately, I could only cook a few types of ramen. So I joined cooking classes to discover more. I have tried a lot of authentic ramen in my life, which allowed me to learn even more about ramen. Now I can make different kinds of ramen without any difficulty. Ramen has various important ingredients. These ingredients are not available everywhere, sometimes you have to make them yourself.

I joined cooking classes and researched a lot in order to learn how to cook different types of ramen. After that, I was able to cook the perfect ramen. This cookbook is not an ordinary cookbook. It is based on many years of experience and effort. I hope you will find it helpful.

The ingredients used in ramen are different than in other noodle meals. The noodles are made from different wheat, and they have a springy quality. But the best thing about ramen is it has no specific rules. If you do not have ramen noodles, you can use normal noodles. I keep the broth in my fridge because it is easy to make and less expensive than buying. The same goes for toppings, sometimes I prepare them myself or buy them from stores. This depends on you and how much time and effort you are prepared to put into your ramen.

The information in this book will help you cook ramen faster and better. Don't be worried if you have never cooked before. All the recipes are self-explanatory. You can follow the steps and make the perfect homemade ramen. It has various types of ramen recipes, so you won't get bored with ramen anytime soon.

The main five ingredients of ramen are broth, tare, aromatic oils, noodles, and toppings. I have also included how to make the toppings for ramen, so you can make them at home and have the proper taste of homemade ramen. All these recipes are personally tested, so you can trust that they will work.

Finally, thank you for reading this cookbook. As an author, this is a big achievement for me. We authors try to help our readers in every way possible. If this cookbook helps you make delicious ramen, please share it with your friends and family. Take care and live a tasty life.

Chapter 1
Basics of Ramen

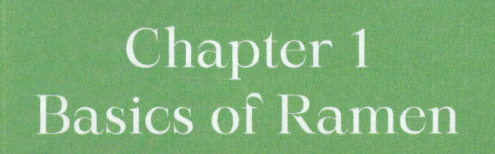

History of Ramen

AN OVERVIEW OF RAMEN'S ORIGIN

Ramen originated in China. The name was originally used for two other dishes, chuka soba, and shina soba, both of which mean 'Chinese noodle'. Japan only adopted the term in the late nineteenth century, during its industrial revolution. However, World War II annihilated ramen's initial popularity. There are numerous theories as to how ramen came to Japan.

THE FIRST JAPANESE RAMEN

In Tokyo, the first ramen shop was established in 1910. Up until the 1950s, it was referred to as shina soba, which is a translation of Chinese soba. Cut noodles, a salty broth made from pork bones, and a few vegetable toppings were included in the initial ramen's preparation. It was served to employees on mobile carts pulled by Chinese immigrants.

RAMEN GOES GLOBAL

Ramen and other Japanese foods were introduced to American troops during World War II. Between 1945 and 1952, when there was a shortage of rice, the U.S. distributed a lot of wheat flour. The flour was utilized by Japanese chefs to make ramen noodles. Ramen was initially offered on the black market at eateries and on yakuza-owned carts. It quickly garnered a lot of popularity and would go on to rank among the most significant Japanese dishes.

When the dish was taken to the U.S. by American troops, it was warmly accepted. In 1958, instant noodles were developed, further enhancing the accessibility of ramen. There are about 5,000 ramen shops in Tokyo, and ramen is a popular Japanese dish all over the world.

RAMEN & VARIATIONS

Thin wheat noodles in a meat broth make up traditional ramen. Ingredients include menma, onions, dried seaweed, and sliced pork. Bean sprouts, maize, BBQ pork, soy sauce, and boiled eggs are a few examples of variations. The flavor of a broth can be made spicy or sweet by adding herbs and spices.

Essential Ingredients for Making a Bowl of Ramen

BROTH

Every good ramen bowl starts with a decent broth. It is the broth that gives the heartwarming aspects of an excellent bowl of ramen. The basic ingredients for the soup are usually comprised of chicken, pig, seafood, and/or vegetables. The secret to making an excellent broth is to draw out flavor and body from the components.

While the body or mouthfeel of the soup is derived from the bones, fat, and connective tissue, the flavor is often extracted from the meat and veggies.

The personalities and hues of ramen broth vary, much like those of the people who drink it. Shio and shoyu ramen frequently contain chintan, also known as "clear soups," which are ingredients that are removed at low temperatures. On the other end of the spectrum, there are paitan, or white soup broths, like tonkotsu ramen or tori paitan. Ingredients need to be heated at higher temperatures to develop their thick and hazy features and to produce emulsions between the higher collagen and fat content.

TARE

The soup's sauce or seasoning, known as tare, adds a lot of umami and saltiness. This is every ramen chef's secret weapon. A few common components include soy sauce, wine, sake, kombu (kelp), niboshi (dried sardines), miso, and salt. Without tare, the broth would simply be meaty soup water.

Tare is frequently used as a preamble to ramen, such as with miso ramen, shoyu ramen, and shio ramen, which uses salt tare.

NOODLES

While the broth is the heart of a bowl of ramen, the noodles set ramen apart from other noodle soup dishes. At their core, ramen noodles are made of kansui, or alkaline water, wheat flour, and water. The noodles' structure is created by the starch and gluten interactions between the water and wheat, and the kansui chemical interacts with the protein in the flour to give the noodles their distinctive chewy texture and yellow color. Salt is frequently used because it reinforces the structure and brings out a little bit of the noodle flavor. Because of their proteins and lipids, eggs, whether they are fresh or powdered, can lend softness and bounce to food.

Getting the ratio just right is the challenging part of creating ramen noodles. Even in Japan, many restaurants purchase noodles. While Hakata Tonkotsu style noodles are pale, straight, and stiff, Tokyo style noodles are bright yellow and curly. The texture and flavor of noodles are determined by the proportion of flour to water, solution, or alkaline salts. It also depends on a lot of other things, such as how much protein is in the flour, how hard the water is, and how the alkaline salts are made. The technique is incredibly difficult for inexperienced cooks, but when done well, it is very satisfying.

TOPPINGS

The most typical ingredients are chashu, green onions, menma (bamboo shoots), seaweed, and the highly regarded ajitsuke tamago (marinated egg).

Everyone has a different preference for how their ramen should be dressed. The majority of eateries let customers add more toppings according to their tastes.

OIL

It's common practice to ignore the oily coating on a bowl of ramen. Garlic and other flavorings can be added to the oil and placed on top of the broth surface. Oil is better able to extract tastes from food than water because of its hydrophobic properties. The flavorful oil coats the noodles as they are submerged in the broth, and as they are swallowed, they acquire a smooth texture. Additionally, serving as insulation, oil keeps the temperature from falling too quickly.

Essential Tools

LARGE STOCKPOT

There will be enough soup in a 10-quart stockpot for most home cooks' needs. Depending on how much ramen you are cooking at once, you might need two stockpots so you can simmer the soup and boil the noodles at the same time.

SAUCEPAN

A 2-quart saucepan comes in handy for cooking just enough soup for two bowls at a time, while the giant stockpot is used to prepare the broth.

DEEP FINE-MESH STRAINER

With a handle for holding, this strainer resembles a saucepan in shape. The surplus water on the noodles is shaken off using these deep metal strainers. Any type of strainer will do, although the deep ones are simpler to shake without the noodles spilling out (a simple approach to ruin all your effort).

A GOOD KNIFE

You should use a good, sharp knife to cut the toppings so that they are neatly and uniformly distributed. It is sufficient to use a chef's knife or a Japanese santoku.

PLASTIC CONTAINERS FOR LIQUIDS AND TOPPINGS

You'll save a lot of time—something you don't have much of while preparing a bowl of ramen—by using small containers to carry your oils, seasoning liquids, and precut garnishes.

KITCHEN SCALE

Many of your ingredients will require weighing. A portable digital scale powered by batteries is simple to use and provides accurate weights in tiny increments.

SPICE GRINDER

You will require this to grind the ingredients in the tares (seasoning liquid). A coffee grinder will serve just fine, but you shouldn't use the same one to grind your coffee and your tare, as this will result in coffee flavors in your tare.

MEASURING SPOONS AND LADLES

You must measure carefully because you must add exactly the right amount of each liquid to a bowl of ramen. For each liquid, use a different measuring spoon or ladle to avoid taste mixing.

Optional Tools

PRESSURE COOKER

Making creamy soups can be done more quickly with a pressure cooker. In a stockpot, creamy tonkotsu pig broths may be simmered for more than 24 hours, but the intense heat of a pressure cooker may extract the collagen from the bones in less than 2 hours.

PASTA MACHINES

If a ramen cafe decides to create their own noodles, they will frequently invest up to $20,000 on a professional-grade noodle machine. More than a hundred servings of noodles are produced every hour by these professional tools. Home appliances, which can range from sophisticated models to straightforward hand-cranked pasta rollers, are far more useful for small quantities. If you want to make your own noodles, you will unquestionably need to have a pasta machine to roll the dough into thin sheets. However, you are fully free to decide how fancy the machine should be.

RAMEN BOWLS AND SPOONS

Ramen-specific ceramic bowls will keep the heat of the soup better. The deep bowl of ramen spoons, which are also made of ceramic, can accommodate a lot of soup and even some toppings. Additionally, they include a tiny hook at the handle's tip that rests on the edge of the bowl and prevents the spoon from getting drenched in your ramen.

CHOPSTICKS

The ideal way to savor a hot bowl of ramen is with a pair of chopsticks, though you can eat it with a fork as well. It's actually simpler than you might think to eat noodles with chopsticks!

PEPPER MILLS

Black pepper is one of the few condiments that may be found on every tabletop in ramen establishments. Pre-ground black pepper is far inferior to freshly ground pepper. White pepper is also available in some stores (it pairs well with creamy soups), while pink peppercorns are occasionally seen.

SESAME-SEED GRINDER

Sesame seeds are intended for use with this specific type of spice grinder. A typical garnish for creamy tonkotsu ramen is ground sesame. A hand-crank variant costs less than $10.

I appreciate you taking the time to read this book and trying the recipes. I sincerely hope that reading the book and experimenting with the recipes will bring you pleasure.

Chapter 2
Broth & Tare

Basic Clear Chicken Soup

Prep Time: 30 minutes plus overnight to soak | **Cook Time:** 4 hours | **Serves 6**

- 1 ounce dried konbu
- 1 dried shiitake mushroom (about 1 ounce)
- 3 quarts water
- 2 pounds chicken parts and/or bones
- 1 tablespoon dry white wine

1. In a large stockpot, soak the konbu and shiitake in the water overnight to make a simple dashi.
2. In a separate large pot, boil enough water to submerge the chicken. Rinse the chicken parts, then plunge them into the boiling water for about 3 seconds. (This essentially cleans the bird, and will mean a lot less scum to skim when cooking the broth.) Remove the chicken and place it in the pot of dashi.
3. Turn the heat to high, and keep an eye on the broth while the temperature rises. Skim off any scum that rises to the surface. Just before the soup begins boiling, lower the heat to a simmer.
4. Using a long-handle slotted spoon, remove the konbu and shiitake mushroom. Add the white wine.
5. Simmer, uncovered, over low heat for 4 hours.
6. Strain the soup into a container, then reheat as necessary for each bowl of ramen.

Traditional Clear Chicken Soup

Prep Time: 30 minutes plus overnight to soak | **Cook Time:** 4 hours | **Serves 8**

- 1 ounce dried konbu
- 1 dried shiitake mushroom (about 1 ounce)
- 4 quarts water
- 4 pounds chicken parts and/or bones
- ½ apple
- 1 teaspoon grated fresh ginger
- 2 garlic cloves, peeled

1. In a large stockpot, soak the konbu and shiitake in the water overnight to make a simple dashi.
2. In a separate large pot, boil enough water to submerge the chicken. Rinse the chicken parts, then plunge them into the boiling water for about 3 seconds. (This essentially cleans the bird, and will mean a lot less scum to skim when cooking the broth.) Remove the chicken and place it in the pot of dashi.
3. Turn the heat to high, and keep an eye on the broth while the temperature rises. Skim off any scum that rises to the surface. Just before the soup begins boiling, lower the heat to a simmer.
4. Using a long-handle slotted spoon, remove the konbu and shiitake. Skim off the scum again, and add the apple half, ginger, and garlic cloves.
5. Simmer, uncovered, over low heat for 4 hours.
6. Strain the soup into a container, then reheat as necessary for each bowl of ramen.

Tonkotsu Creamy Soup
Prep Time: 20 minutes | Cook Time: 1 hour | Serves 5

- 7 pounds pork bones or pig trotters
- 5 quarts water (but not more than the water-limit line of your pressure cooker)
- 8 ounces chicken bones or chicken meat
- 8 ounces potatoes, peeled and halved

1. Put all the ingredients in the pressure cooker. Seal the cooker and heat to high pressure.
2. Cook at high pressure for 30 minutes. Release the pressure by turning off the heat and allowing the steam to vent. Remove the lid and stir the soup.
3. with the pot uncovered, turn the heat to high. Continuously stir the soup for about 10 minutes, until it becomes white and creamy.
4. Remove from the heat and strain the soup through a fine-mesh strainer. Reheat as necessary for each bowl of ramen.

Basic Chicken Broth
Prep Time: 15 minutes | Cook Time: 6 hours | Serves 8

- 3 pounds chicken bones
- 1 pound chicken feet, blanched, drained, and rinsed
- 1 pound chicken wings
- 10 to 12 cups water

1. In a large stockpot, put the chicken bones, feet, and wings, and add the water. Set the pot over low heat, bring to a simmer, and skim off any foam that rises to the top. Cover the pot and simmer for 6 hours.
2. Place a strainer or colander over a large bowl, pour the broth into it, and discard the solids.
3. Let the broth cool to room temperature and then refrigerate it for at least 4 hours.
4. Skim the fat off the top of the broth (if you'd like, you can save it and use it to season your ramen or as a cooking fat).

Mushroom Broth
Prep Time: 5 minutes | Cook Time: 5 minutes plus 30 minutes to let rest | Serves 8

- 8 cups water
- 3 ounces dried shiitake mushrooms, stemmed and cut into strips

1. In a stockpot, combine the water and dried mushrooms, and over medium-high heat bring to a simmer.
2. Remove the pot from the heat and let stand for about 30 minutes.
3. Strain the mushrooms out of the broth. (Save the mushrooms and add them to your soup, if desired.)

Kare (Curry) Coconut Tare

Prep Time: 10 minutes | Cook Time: 10 minutes | Serves 4

- 1 (14-ounce) can coconut milk
- ¼ cup mirin
- ¼ ounce (4-inch square) konbu
- 2 scallions, green and white parts, roughly chopped
- 3 garlic cloves, crushed and chopped
- 1 tablespoon (1-inch piece) fresh ginger, unpeeled, crushed, and chopped
- 2 tablespoons Japanese curry powder
- 1 teaspoon spicy sesame oil
- 1 tablespoon white miso
- 2 tablespoons dark brown sugar, packed

1. In a medium saucepan over high heat, bring the coconut milk, mirin, konbu, and scallions to a low simmer.
2. Whisk in the garlic, ginger, curry powder, sesame oil, miso, and brown sugar and simmer for 10 minutes.
3. Using a fine-mesh strainer, filter the broth and discard the solids. Serve.

Basic Beef Broth

Prep Time: 15 minutes | Cook Time: 10 hours | Serves 8

- 4 to 5 pounds beef bones, cut into 2- to 3-inch pieces, blanched, drained, and rinsed
- 1 onion, peeled and halved
- 12 to 16 cups water

1. In a large stockpot, combine the beef bones, onion, and water. Bring to a boil over high heat. Reduce the heat to medium and skim off the brown foam that rises to the top, then cook at a hearty simmer for 8 hours. To keep the bones covered, add water if needed.
2. Raise the heat to high and bring to a rolling boil. Cook at a hard boil, occasionally stirring vigorously with a wooden spoon, for another 1 to 2 hours.
3. Place a strainer or colander over a large bowl, pour the broth into it, and discard the solids.
4. Let the broth cool to room temperature and then refrigerate it for at least 4 hours.
5. Skim the fat off the top of the broth (if you'd like, you can save it and use it to season your ramen or as a cooking fat)

Shoyu Tare

Prep Time: 10 minutes | Cook Time: 10 minutes | Serves 4

- 1 cup soy sauce or tamari
- ½ cup mirin
- ¼ cup dark brown sugar, packed
- 6 garlic cloves, crushed and chopped
- 1 tablespoon (1-inch piece) fresh ginger, unpeeled, crushed, and chopped
- 6 scallions, green and white parts, roughly chopped
- 1 teaspoon spicy sesame oil

1. In a medium saucepan over medium-high heat, combine the soy sauce, mirin, brown sugar, garlic, ginger, scallions, and sesame oil and bring to a boil.
2. Reduce the heat to medium and continue boiling and stirring for 10 minutes.
3. Using a fine-mesh strainer, filter the broth and discard the solids. Serve.

Spicy Miso Tare

Prep Time: 5 minutes | Cook Time: 5 minutes | Serves 2

- ⅓ cup chili paste or gochujang (Korean fermented chili paste)
- ¼ cup white miso
- ¼ cup red miso
- ¼ cup kosher salt
- ¼ cup water
- 3 tablespoons Japanese sesame paste
- 2 tablespoons sesame oil
- 1 tablespoon rice wine vinegar
- 1 tablespoon grated fresh ginger

1. In a medium mixing bowl, combine the chili paste, white and red miso, salt, water, Japanese sesame paste, sesame oil, rice wine vinegar, and ginger, and stir to mix well.
2. Store in an airtight container in the refrigerator for up to 3 weeks or in the freezer for up to 3 months.

Ramen For Beginners | 13

Chapter 3
Toppings

Pork Chashu

Prep Time: 20 minutes | Cook Time: 35 minutes | Serves 6

- 1 pound boneless pork belly or shoulder
- Salt
- Freshly ground black pepper
- 2 cups soy sauce
- ¾ cup honey
- ½ cup dry white wine

1. Season the pork with a little salt and pepper.
2. Heat a large skillet over medium heat. When it's hot, add the pork and brown the meat on all sides.
3. Transfer the browned pork to a large stockpot and add the soy sauce, honey, and white wine.
4. Bring to a boil over high heat, then reduce the heat to medium and simmer, uncovered, for 25 minutes.
5. Remove from the heat and let cool to room temperature. To let the flavors soak in evenly, rotate the pork in the seasoning liquid every 10 minutes or so while it's cooling. To make this easier, cover the top of the pork with a heavy-duty paper towel; the paper will help the liquid soak evenly into the meat.
6. Once the pork is cooled to room temperature, remove it from the seasoning liquid and discard the paper towels. The pork can be cut and used immediately, or wrapped in plastic wrap and stored in the refrigerator for a few days.

Chicken Chashu

Prep Time: 20 minutes | Cook Time: 35 minutes | Serves 6

- 1 pound boneless, skin-on chicken thighs
- 2½ cups water
- 2 cups soy sauce
- ½ cup dry white wine
- ¾ cup sugar

1. Roll the chicken thighs, skin-side out, into tight rolls, and secure with cooking twine. (Tie the twine with a bow that can be easily untied later.)
2. Heat a large skillet over medium heat. When it's hot, add the chicken and brown the meat on all sides.
3. In a large stockpot, combine the water, soy sauce, white wine, and sugar. Stir to dissolve the sugar completely, then add the chicken.
4. Bring to a boil over high heat, then reduce the heat to medium and simmer, uncovered, for 25 minutes.
5. Remove from the heat and let cool to room temperature. To let the flavors soak in evenly, rotate the chicken in the seasoning liquid every 10 minutes or so while it's cooling. To make this easier, cover the top of the chicken with a heavy-duty paper towel; the paper will help the liquid evenly soak into the meat.
6. Once the chicken is cooled to room temperature, remove it from the seasoning liquid and discard the paper towels. The chicken can be cut and used immediately, or wrapped in plastic wrap and stored in the refrigerator for a few days.

Niku Soboro (Minced Meat Topping)
Prep Time: 15 minutes | Cook Time: 15 minutes | Serves 6

- 1 pound minced pork, chicken, or beef
- Salt
- Freshly ground black pepper
- ½ cup tianmianjiang (Chinese sweet bean paste)
- Pinch chile pepper flakes or minced fresh chile pepper

1. In a large skillet, stir-fry the minced meat over medium-high heat with a little salt and pepper.
2. When the meat is fully cooked, stir in the sweet bean paste.
3. Remove from the heat and add the chile pepper. Mix well.
4. Use immediately or store in an airtight container in the refrigerator for a few days.

Negi (Scallion) Oil
Prep Time: 10 minutes | Cook Time: 5 minutes | Serves 1½ cups

- 1½ cups lard (pork fat) or vegetable oil
- ¼ cup roughly chopped scallions (green parts only)

1. In a medium saucepan, heat the lard over medium heat to melt it.
2. Add the scallions and cook for a few minutes, stirring, until they turn light brown.
3. Take the pan off the heat and strain the negi oil into a container. Discard the scallion pieces.
4. Store in an airtight container in the refrigerator for up to 6 months.

Seasoned Bamboo Shoots
Prep Time: 5 minutes | Cook Time: 20 minutes | Serves 2 cups

- 8 ounces fresh bamboo shoots, cut into strips
- 1 cup Basic Vegan Broth or water
- 1½ teaspoons sesame oil
- 1½ teaspoons soy sauce
- 1½ teaspoons sake or rice wine
- 1½ teaspoons sugar
- ½ teaspoon kosher salt

1. In a medium saucepan, combine the bamboo shoots, broth, sesame oil, soy sauce, sake, sugar, and salt, and bring to a boil over high heat.
2. Reduce the heat to medium and simmer the mixture for about 20 minutes, until the liquid has mostly evaporated.

Roasted Tomatoes

Prep Time: 10 minutes | Cook Time: 30 minutes | Serves 24 tomato halves

- 12 plum tomatoes, halved
- 3 tablespoons extra-virgin olive oil
- 1 teaspoon kosher salt
- ½ teaspoon freshly ground black pepper

1. Preheat the oven to 450°F.
2. In a bowl, toss the tomatoes and olive oil together to coat the tomatoes well. Arrange the tomatoes on a large rimmed baking sheet, cut-side up. Sprinkle the tomatoes with the salt and pepper.
3. Roast the tomatoes for about 30 minutes, until they are very tender and are beginning to brown on the edges.

Ajitama Eggs

Prep Time: 5 minutes | Cook Time: 9 minutes plus overnight to marinate | Serves 4

- 3 cups water
- 4 large eggs, at room temperature
- 3 cups ice water
- 1 cup soy sauce
- ¼ cup mirin
- 2 tablespoons dark brown sugar, packed

1. In a medium pot over high heat, bring enough water to cover the eggs by 1 inch to a boil.
2. Gently lower the eggs into the boiling water and cook for 5 to 9 minutes, depending on the size of the eggs.
3. Remove the eggs and immediately put them into a bowl with the ice water to stop the cooking process.
4. In a medium bowl, combine the soy sauce, mirin, and brown sugar. Once cooled, peel the eggs and marinate them in the soy sauce mixture. Cover the bowl with a paper towel; refrigerate overnight.
5. Halve the eggs before adding to the ramen bowls.

Marinated Bean Sprouts

Prep Time: 10 minutes | Cook Time: 5 minutes plus 15 minutes to let rest | Serves 2 cups

- 1 cup water
- 12 ounces bean sprouts
- 2 tablespoons sesame oil
- 1½ teaspoons soy sauce
- ½ teaspoon kosher salt
- ¼ teaspoon freshly ground black pepper
- ¼ teaspoon red pepper flakes
- 2 scallions, both white and green parts, thinly sliced
- 1 tablespoon toasted sesame seeds

1. In a medium saucepan, bring the water to a boil. Add the bean sprouts and cook for about 30 seconds. Drain in a colander and rinse well with cold water. Press down on the sprouts to remove excess water.
2. In a medium bowl, whisk together the sesame oil, soy sauce, salt, pepper, and red pepper flakes. Stir in the scallions, sesame seeds, and bean sprouts. Let the sprouts stand for at least 15 minutes, then serve.

La-Yu Chili Oil

Prep Time: 10 minutes | Cook Time: 10 minutes | Serves 1 cup

- ½ cup neutral-flavored oil (such as canola, vegetable, peanut, or avocado)
- 2 garlic cloves, crushed and chopped
- 1 tablespoon (1-inch piece) fresh ginger, unpeeled, crushed, and chopped
- 1 scallion, green and white parts, roughly chopped
- 1 tablespoon red chili flakes or ¼ cup chopped fresh hot peppers
- ¼ cup toasted sesame oil

1. In a saucepan over medium heat, combine the neutral oil, garlic, ginger, scallion, and red chili flakes. Cook, stirring frequently, for 10 minutes.
2. Remove the saucepan from the heat and stir in the sesame oil. Cool to room temperature before straining the oil into an airtight container. Discard the solids.

Mayu (Black Garlic Paste)

Prep Time: 5 minutes | Cook Time: 15 minutes | Serves 1 cup

- ¼ cup vegetable oil
- 10 garlic cloves, crushed and chopped
- 1 tablespoon (1-inch piece) fresh ginger, unpeeled, crushed, and chopped
- ¼ cup toasted sesame oil
- 2 tablespoons soy sauce or tamari

1. In a medium saucepan over medium heat, combine the vegetable oil, garlic, and ginger. Sauté until the garlic begins to turn light brown, stirring occasionally to ensure even browning.
2. Reduce the heat to low and cook until the garlic turns dark brown, about 15 minutes.
3. Remove from the heat and stir in the sesame oil and soy sauce.
4. Transfer to an airtight container and refrigerate for up to 3 months.

Ginger Pork

Prep Time: 5 minutes | Cook Time: 6 minutes | Serves 4

- 1 pound ground pork
- ½ teaspoon salt
- 1 garlic clove, minced
- 1 (2-inch) piece fresh ginger, peeled and minced
- 1 teaspoon soy sauce

1. Heat a large skillet over medium-high heat. Add the pork and salt and cook, stirring occasionally and breaking up with a spatula, until the meat is browned, about 5 minutes.
2. Add the garlic and ginger and cook, stirring, for 1 minute more. Stir in the soy sauce and remove from the heat.

Chicken Karaage

Prep Time: 10 minutes plus 30 minutes to marinate | **Cook Time:** 5 minutes | **Serves 4**

- 1 pound boneless, skinless chicken thighs, cut into 2-inch pieces
- 2 tablespoons soy sauce
- 1 tablespoon sake
- 1 teaspoon sesame oil
- 1 teaspoon grated fresh ginger
- 1 teaspoon sugar
- Neutral-flavored vegetable oil, for deep-frying
- ½ cup potato starch
- ¼ teaspoon kosher salt
- ½ teaspoon freshly ground black pepper

1. Pat the chicken pieces dry with paper towels.
2. In a medium bowl, combine the soy sauce, sake, sesame oil, ginger, and sugar. Stir to mix. Add the chicken and toss to coat. Let marinate in the refrigerator for at least 30 minutes or as long as overnight.
3. Fill a deep saucepan with about 3 inches of vegetable oil (using a deep pot helps contain the splatter) and heat over high heat until it shimmers.
4. In a wide shallow bowl, stir together the potato starch, salt, and pepper. Lift the chicken pieces out of the marinade and dredge in the potato starch mixture, turning thoroughly to coat.
5. Gently lower the chicken pieces into the hot oil and cook until they are golden brown and float to the top, about 3 minutes, turning to ensure they brown all over. Transfer to a paper towel–lined plate and let cool for a few minutes before returning them to the oil to cook for another minute or so, until they are a deep golden brown. Transfer to another paper towel–lined plate to drain off excess oil.

Teriyaki Pork Tenderloin

Prep Time: 15 minutes | **Cook Time:** 30 minutes | **Serves 4**

- 1/4 cup soy sauce
- 1/4 cup mirin
- 1 tablespoon brown sugar
- 1/2 cup water
- 1 tablespoon vegetable oil
- 1 1/2 lbs pork tenderloin, rinse and pat dry with paper towels

1. Mix brown sugar, mirin, soy sauce, and water in a bowl.
2. Heat oil in a deep fry pan. Brown each side of pork tenderloin for 5 minutes.
3. Pour the sauce into the pan. Cover with lid, switch heat to medium low and cook for 30 minutes, turning once half way through. If needed, add another 1/4 cup water to avoid burning.
4. Remove pork from pan and slice after it has cooled enough.

Soy Sauce Eggs

Prep Time: 5 minutes plus 10 hours to marinate | Cook Time: 4 minutes | Serves 6

- ¾ cup shoyu or low-sodium soy sauce
- ½ cup sake
- ¼ cup mirin
- ¾ cup warm water
- 1 tablespoon sugar
- 2 teaspoons chopped fresh ginger
- 6 Soft-Boiled Eggs, chilled and peeled

1. In a saucepan, combine the shoyu, sake, mirin, water, sugar, and ginger. Bring to a boil over high heat, then reduce to medium-low and simmer, stirring frequently, until the sugar is completely dissolved, about 3 to 4 minutes. Transfer to a jar or container large enough to fit both the eggs and the liquid, and let cool.
2. Add the peeled eggs to the cooled shoyu mixture and let marinate in the refrigerator for 8 to 10 hours (no longer than 12 hours or the eggs will become rubbery). Remove the eggs from the marinade and keep them in a bowl or jar, covered, in the refrigerator until ready to use. The eggs will keep in the refrigerator for up to 3 days.
3. To serve, slice the eggs in half lengthwise and float 1 or 2 halves on top of a bowl of ramen.

Shio Kakuni Pork

Prep Time: 10 minutes | Cook Time: 2 hours | Serves 6

- 3 lb pork belly
- 5 oz scallions, cut into 4-inch pieces
- 1 1/2-inch length fresh ginger, sliced into coins
- 4 large cloves garlic
- 0.35 oz niboshi
- 3 cups water
- 3/4 cups sake
- 3 tablespoons evaporated cane sugar
- 2 tablespoons soy sauce
- 2 teaspoons salt

1. Bring water to a boil and add pork belly. Lower the heat and simmer for 30 minutes.
2. Drain, rinse out the pot, and scrub all coagulated proteins off the meat surface.
3. Cut pork into 2-inch cubes and return them to the pot, then add remaining ingredients.
4. When boiling, turn to low and simmer for 1 hour 30 minutes, partially covering with a lid.

Menma

Prep Time: 10 minutes | **Cook Time:** 30 minutes | **Serves 6**

- 1/2 cup bamboo shoots
- 2 cups water
- 1/2 cup teriyaki sauce or Chashu seasonings
- 1/4 cup mirin
- 1 handful bonito flakes

1. Mix bamboo shoots, water, teriyaki and mirin in a saucepan.
2. Bring to a boil, then add bonito flakes and reduce heat. Let simmer for 25 minutes.
3. Turn off heat and let it cool.
4. Transfer shoots and liquid to an airtight container and refrigerate overnight.
5. Can be stored in the fridge for a week.

Pickled Daikon Radish

Prep Time: 10 minutes plus 2 hours to drain and 2 days to cure | **Cook Time:** 5 minutes | **Serves 1 pint**

- 1 daikon radish, peeled and sliced into thin rounds
- 1 tablespoon salt
- ½ cup sugar
- ½ cup water
- ½ cup rice wine vinegar
- 1 teaspoon ground turmeric

1. Toss the daikon rounds with the salt and let stand in a colander (set over a bowl or in the sink) for about 2 hours.
2. In a medium saucepan over medium-high heat, combine the sugar, water, rice wine vinegar, and turmeric and bring to a boil. Cook, stirring, until the sugar dissolves, about 3 minutes.
3. Squeeze any excess water from the daikon and transfer to a heat-safe jar or bowl. Pour the hot pickling liquid over the top. Cover and refrigerate for at least 2 days.
4. Pickled Daikon Radish will keep in the refrigerator for at least 1 month.

Roasted Kabocha Squash
Prep Time: 5 minutes | **Cook Time:** 30 minutes | **Serves 4**

- 1 tablespoon white miso
- 2 teaspoons soy sauce
- 1 tablespoon neutral-flavored vegetable oil
- 2 teaspoons brown sugar
- ½ kabocha squash, peeled, seeded, and cut into cubes

1. Preheat the oven to 400°F.
2. In a medium bowl, stir together the miso, soy sauce, oil, and brown sugar to combine well. Add the squash and toss to coat.
3. Spread the squash out in a single layer on a baking sheet and roast in the oven for 25 to 30 minutes, until tender and beginning to brown.

Tamagoyaki (Japanese Omelet)
Prep Time: 5 minutes | **Cook Time:** 10 minutes | **Serves 1**

- 4 eggs
- 1 tablespoon soy sauce
- 1 tablespoon mirin
- 1 tablespoon sugar
- 1 pinch of salt
- cooking oil, as needed

1. Beat eggs well in a bowl using a fork, or chopsticks.
2. Add soy sauce, mirin, sugar and salt to the egg mixture.
3. Add cooking oil to a pan and bring it up to medium heat. Keep some paper towels handy to help keep the pan oiled during cooking.
4. Pour a little of egg mixture into the heated pan. Once it has cooked slightly and the top is still slightly uncooked, push it over to the other side of pan.
5. Oil the pan with a paper towel and add another small amount of the egg mixture to the pan. Wait until it's cooked a little, but before set on top, and roll the first bit of egg over the mixture that has been just put in the pan until you get a small roll of egg. Keep adding the egg in new layers until you have used it all up.
6. Remove and let it cool before slicing.

Ebi Abura (Shrimp Oil)

Prep Time: 10 minutes | **Cook Time:** 5 minutes | **Serves 1/2 cup**

- ¼ cup dried shrimp or dried shrimp powder
- ½ cup vegetable oil

1. If the dried shrimp are whole, use a blender or spice grinder to grind them into a fine powder.
2. In a small saucepan, combine the shrimp powder and vegetable oil.
3. Heat over high heat, stirring to mix, for a few minutes.
4. Cool and transfer to a glass jar. Store in an airtight container in the refrigerator for up to 6 months.

Sesame Paste

Prep Time: 10 minutes | **Cook Time:** 5 minutes | **Serves 1.5 cups**

- ½ cup roasted white or black sesame seeds
- 1 cup sesame oil

1. Blend the sesame seeds in a blender or spice grinder to make a powder. Transfer the sesame powder in a deep saucepan.
2. In a small skillet, heat the sesame oil over medium-high heat until it is smoking hot.
3. Carefully add the hot sesame oil little by little to the sesame powder, taking care not to splatter the hot oil. Mix well.
4. Cool and transfer to a glass jar. Store in an airtight container in the refrigerator for up to 6 months.

Chapter 4
Shio Ramen

Basic Shio Ramen

Prep Time: 10 minutes | Cook Time: 10 minutes | Serves 4

- ½ cup Shio Tare
- 5 cups Basic Clear Chicken Soup
- 1⅓ pounds fresh noodles, such as Chukasuimen
- 4 to 8 slices Chicken Chashu
- Negi

1. with all your ingredients ready to go, bring a large pot of water to a boil over medium-high heat.
2. Heat your ramen bowls by filling them halfway with hot water. The bowls don't need to be scalding, but they should be hot to the touch. Dump out the hot water and dry the bowls with some paper towels or a clean towel.
3. Put the tare and soup in a medium saucepan. Mix and bring to a simmer over low heat.
4. Cook the noodles in the large pot of boiling water. Ramen that has been cut to a standard thickness (about 1 mm) will cook in 1 to 2 minutes.
5. About 30 seconds before the noodles are finished cooking, ladle the soup into the ramen bowls.
6. Drain the noodles, taking care to shake off as much excess water as you can. Carefully place some noodles in each bowl of soup, keeping them tidy.
7. Place a slice or two of chicken chashu and a sprinkle of negi neatly on the ramen. Serve immediately.

Traditional Shio Ramen

Prep Time: 10 minutes | Cook Time: 10 minutes | Serves 4

- ½ cup Shio Tare
- 5 cups any type clear soup (here, here, here, here)
- 1⅓ pounds fresh noodles, such as Chukasuimen (here)
- 4 to 8 slices Chicken Chashu
- 12 to 16 pieces Menma
- 4 Salted Eggs, halved
- Negi

1. with all your ingredients ready to go, bring a large pot of water to a boil over medium-high heat.
2. Heat your ramen bowls by filling them halfway with hot water. The bowls don't need to be scalding, but they should be hot to the touch. Dump out the hot water and dry the bowls with some paper towels or a clean towel.
3. Put the tare and soup in a medium saucepan. Mix and bring to a simmer over low heat.
4. Cook the noodles in the large pot of boiling water. Ramen that has been cut to a standard thickness (about 1 mm) will cook in 1 to 2 minutes.
5. About 30 seconds before the noodles are finished cooking, ladle the soup into the ramen bowls.
6. Drain the noodles, taking care to shake off as much excess water as you can. Carefully place some noodles in each bowl of soup, keeping them tidy.
7. Place 1 or 2 slices of chashu, 3 or 4 slices of menma, a salted egg, and a sprinkle of negi neatly on the ramen. Serve immediately.

Green Vegetable Shio Ramen

Prep Time: 10 minutes | Cook Time: 10 minutes | Serves 4

- ½ cup Vegetarian Shio Tare
- 5 cups Vegetarian Clear Soup
- 1⅓ pounds fresh noodles, such as Chukasuimen
- 12 to 16 pieces Menma
- Green Vegetable Topping
- Negi

1. with all your ingredients ready to go, bring a large pot of water to a boil over medium-high heat.
2. Heat your ramen bowls by filling them halfway with hot water. The bowls don't need to be scalding, but they should be hot to the touch. Dump out the hot water and dry the bowls with some paper towels or a clean towel.
3. Put the tare and soup in a medium saucepan. Mix and bring to a simmer over low heat.
4. Cook the noodles in the large pot of boiling water. Ramen that has been cut to a standard thickness (about 1 mm) will cook in 1 to 2 minutes.
5. About 30 seconds before the noodles are finished cooking, ladle the soup into the ramen bowls.
6. Drain the noodles, taking care to shake off as much excess water as you can. Carefully place some noodles in each bowl of soup, keeping them tidy.
7. Place 3 or 4 slices of menma, some cooked green vegetables, and a sprinkle of negi neatly on the ramen. Serve immediately.

Shio Ramen with Corn, Roasted Tomatoes, and Basil

Prep Time: 15 minutes | Cook Time: 15 minutes | Serves 4

- ½ cup Shio Tare
- 4 teaspoons Scallion Oil
- 8 cups Awase Dashi
- 18 ounces Basic Ramen Noodles (or store-bought) or 12 ounces dried ramen noodles
- Roasted Tomatoes
- 1 cup fresh corn kernels (from 2 ears of corn)
- ¼ cup julienned fresh basil

1. Spoon 2 tablespoons of the tare into each of 4 serving bowls. Add 1 teaspoon of Scallion Oil to each.
2. In a large saucepan, heat the Awase Dashi over high heat until it is just about to boil.
3. Cook the noodles according to the recipe (or package instructions) and then drain well.
4. When the noodles are done cooking, immediately ladle the hot soup into the serving bowls over the tare and oil. Add ¼ of the noodles to each bowl. Stir gently and lift with chopsticks to distribute the tare into the broth and to coat the noodles. The noodles should float on top somewhat.
5. Top each bowl with 2 or 3 tomato halves, ¼ cup of the corn, and 1 tablespoon of basil. Serve immediately

Shio Ramen with Ginger Chicken and Bok Choy

Prep Time: 15 minutes plus 15 minutes to marinate | **Cook Time:** 10 minutes | **Serves 4**

- 2 tablespoons soy sauce
- 2 tablespoons sake
- 2 tablespoons honey
- 1 tablespoon peeled, grated fresh ginger
- 1 pound boneless, skinless chicken thighs, cut into bite-size pieces
- 1 tablespoon cooking oil
- 8 cups Basic Chicken Broth or store-bought broth
- 8 to 12 baby bok choy
- ½ cup Basic Shio Tare
- 18 ounces fresh ramen noodles, 12 ounces dried ramen noodles, or 2 packages instant ramen noodles, cooked according to package directions
- 8 ounces fresh shiitake mushrooms, sliced

1. In a medium bowl, whisk together the soy sauce, sake, honey, and ginger. Add the chicken pieces and toss to coat them well. Marinate the chicken for 15 to 20 minutes.
2. In a medium skillet, heat the oil over medium-high heat. Add the chicken to the pan, discarding the marinade, and cook, stirring occasionally, until the chicken is cooked through and golden brown, 4 minutes.
3. In a pot, heat the broth over medium-high heat until simmering. Add the bok choy and cook for 3 to 4 minutes, until wilted.
4. Into each of 4 serving bowls, put 2 tablespoons of tare. Divide the noodles among the bowls and ladle the broth over the noodles. Divide the bok choy, chicken, and mushrooms among the bowls and serve immediately.

Shio Ramen with Crispy Pork Belly, Scallions, Seasoned Bamboo Shoots, and Nori

Prep Time: 15 minutes | **Cook Time:** 2 hours 45 minutes | **Serves 4**

- For the pork
- 1 pound pork belly, skin-on
- 1 tablespoon cooking oil
- Kosher salt
- Freshly ground black pepper
- For the soup
- 8 cups Basic Pork Broth or store-bought broth
- ½ cup Basic Shio Tare
- 18 ounces fresh ramen noodles, 12 ounces dried ramen noodles, or 2 packages instant ramen noodles, cooked according to package directions
- 4 scallions, both white and green parts, thinly sliced
- ½ cup Seasoned Bamboo Shoots or canned sliced bamboo shoots
- 1 sheet nori, cut into strips

1. Preheat the oven to 350°F and put a wire rack on top of a baking sheet.
2. Score the skin of the pork belly with a very sharp knife, making several small cuts into the skin and fat layer without puncturing the meat. Rub the oil all over the meat and then season it generously with salt and pepper.
3. Place the meat on the rack on top of the baking sheet, skin-side up, and roast for 2½ hours.
4. Raise the heat to 450°F and roast for 15 minutes more.
5. Remove the meat from the oven and let it stand for 15 minutes. Cut the cooked pork belly into ¼-inch-thick slices.
6. In a pot, heat the broth over medium-high heat until simmering.
7. Into each of 4 serving bowls, put 2 tablespoons of tare. Divide the noodles among the bowls and ladle the broth over the noodles. Divide the pork, scallions, bamboo shoots, and nori strips among the bowls. Serve immediately.

Shio Ramen with Ham and Shiitake Mushrooms
Prep Time: 10 minutes | Cook Time: 10 minutes | Serves 4

- 8 cups Basic Pork Broth or store-bought broth
- 2 teaspoons cooking oil
- 12 ounces thickly sliced cooked ham, diced
- 4 ounces shiitake mushrooms, sliced
- Pinch salt
- ½ cup Basic Shio Tare
- 18 ounces fresh ramen noodles, 12 ounces dried ramen noodles, or 2 packages instant ramen noodles, cooked according to package directions
- 4 scallions, both white and green parts, thinly sliced
- 2 Soft-Boiled Eggs, halved

1. In a stockpot, heat the broth over medium-high heat until simmering.
2. In a medium skillet, heat the oil over medium-high heat. Add the ham and cook for 4 minutes, stirring occasionally, until heated through and browned in spots. Transfer the ham to a bowl or plate.
3. In the same skillet, cook the mushrooms with a pinch of salt for 3 to 4 minutes, stirring occasionally, until tender.
4. Into each of 4 serving bowls, put 2 tablespoons of tare. Divide the noodles among the bowls and ladle the broth over the noodles. Divide the ham, mushrooms, and scallions among the bowls and place half an egg on top of each bowl. Serve immediately.

Shio Ramen with Buttery Clams
Prep Time: 10 minutes | Cook Time: 10 minutes | Serves 4

- 1 pound live littleneck clams, cleaned
- 8 cups Basic Fish Broth
- ½ cup Basic Shio Tare
- 18 ounces fresh ramen noodles, 12 ounces dried ramen noodles, or 2 packages instant ramen noodles, cooked according to package directions
- ¼ cup (½ stick) butter, cut into small pieces
- 4 scallions, both white and green parts, thinly sliced

1. Fill a medium saucepan with about 4 inches of water and bring it to a boil over high heat.
2. Add the clams, reduce the heat to medium, cover, and cook for about 10 minutes. The clam shells will open as they cook. Using a slotted spoon, remove the clams carefully from the water. Discard any clams that do not open.
3. In a pot, heat the broth over medium-high heat until simmering.
4. Into each of 4 serving bowls, put 2 tablespoons of tare. Divide the noodles among the bowls and ladle the broth over the noodles. Arrange several clams on top of each bowl and top each clam with a bit of butter. Garnish with the scallions and serve immediately.

Shio Ramen with Shredded Pork and Sesame-Chili Oil

Prep Time: 15 minutes | **Cook Time:** 6 hours (slow cooker) or 1 hour (pressure cooker) | **Serves 4**

- For the pork
- 1 (3½- to 4-pound) pork shoulder, cut into a few large pieces
- 1 teaspoon kosher salt
- 1 cup water
- 1 onion, diced
- ½ cup soy sauce
- ¼ cup sake
- ¼ cup brown sugar
- 6 garlic cloves, minced
- 1-inch piece fresh ginger, peeled and sliced
- For the soup
- 8 cups Basic Pork Broth or store-bought broth
- ½ cup Basic Shio Tare
- 18 ounces fresh ramen noodles, 12 ounces dried ramen noodles, or 2 packages instant ramen noodles, cooked according to package directions
- 4 scallions, both white and green parts, thinly sliced
- 4 teaspoons Sesame-Chili Oil or store-bought chili oil

1. Put the pork into a slow cooker or pressure cooker, and season it all over with the salt.
2. In a medium bowl, stir together the water, onion, soy sauce, sake, sugar, garlic, and ginger. Pour the mixture over the meat.
3. If using a slow cooker, cover and cook on high for 6 hours. If using a pressure cooker, cover, turn the valve to the sealing position, and pressure cook for 1 hour. When the cooking time is up, let the pressure release naturally.
4. When the meat is cooked, it should be very tender and shred easily with a fork. Transfer the meat to a medium bowl and let it rest for 15 minutes or so before shredding it with two forks.
5. In a pot, heat the broth over medium-high heat until simmering.
6. Into each of 4 serving bowls, put 2 tablespoons of tare. Divide the noodles among the bowls and ladle the broth over the noodles. Pile some of the cooked pork on top of each bowl and top it with the scallions. Drizzle 1 teaspoon of chili oil over each bowl and serve immediately

Shio Ramen with 5-Spice Beef Short Ribs

Prep Time: 10 minutes | **Cook Time:** 4 hours 10 minutes | **Serves 4**

- ¼ cup sugar
- 3 tablespoons rice vinegar
- 3 cups Basic Beef Broth or store-bought broth
- ¼ cup soy sauce
- 2 pounds bone-in short ribs, cut into 2-inch pieces
- 5 garlic cloves, peeled
- 3 scallions, both white and green parts, halved lengthwise
- 2-inch piece fresh ginger, peeled and thinly sliced
- 1 teaspoon Chinese five-spice powder
- 8 cups Basic Beef Broth or store-bought broth
- ½ cup Basic Shio Tare
- 18 ounces fresh ramen noodles, 12 ounces dried ramen noodles, or 2 packages instant ramen noodles, cooked according to package directions
- 1 cup radish sprouts or mung bean sprouts
- 4 teaspoons Sesame-Chili Oil or store-bought chili oil

1. In a large saucepan or Dutch oven, heat the sugar and vinegar over medium-high heat for 5 minutes, stirring, until the sugar dissolves and the mixture becomes syrupy. Stir in the broth and soy sauce.
2. Add the ribs, garlic, scallions, ginger, and five-spice powder. Reduce the heat to low, cover the pot, and simmer for about 4 hours, until the meat is very tender.
3. In a pot, heat the broth over medium-high heat until simmering.
4. Into each of 4 serving bowls, put 2 tablespoons of tare. Divide the noodles among the bowls and ladle the broth over the noodles. Divide the meat and sprouts among the bowls. Drizzle the sesame-chili oil over the top and serve immediately.

Scallion-Flavored Shio Ramen

Prep Time: 10 minutes | **Cook Time:** 10 minutes | **Serves 4**

- ½ cup Shio Tare
- 5 cups any type clear soup (here, here, here, here)
- 1⅓ pounds fresh noodles, such as Chukasuimen
- 4 to 6 tablespoons Negi Oil
- 4 cups chopped scallion
- 4 Salted Eggs, halved

1. with all your ingredients ready to go, bring a large pot of water to a boil over medium-high heat.
2. Heat your ramen bowls by filling them halfway with hot water. The bowls don't need to be scalding, but they should be hot to the touch. Dump out the hot water and dry the bowls with some paper towels or a clean towel.
3. Put the tare and soup in a medium saucepan. Mix and bring to a simmer over low heat.
4. Put 1 tablespoon of negi oil in each ramen bowl.
5. About 30 seconds before the noodles are finished cooking, ladle the soup into the ramen bowls.
6. Drain the noodles, taking care to shake off as much excess water as you can. Carefully place some noodles in each bowl of soup, keeping them tidy.
7. Place 1 cup of chopped scallions and 1 salted egg neatly on the ramen. (The scallions should almost cover the entire bowl.) Drizzle with an extra bit of negi oil, if desired. Serve immediately.

Shio Ramen with Curried Beef with Peas and Carrots

Prep Time: 10 minutes | **Cook Time:** 15 minutes | **Serves 4**

- 2 tablespoons cooking oil
- 1 pound top sirloin, thinly sliced
- 4 cups Basic Chicken Broth, Basic Beef Broth, or store-bought broth
- 1 (8-ounce) package Japanese curry mix
- 2 carrots, peeled and diced
- 1 cup frozen peas
- 8 cups Basic Beef Broth or store-bought broth
- ½ cup Basic Shio Tare
- 2 Soft-Boiled Eggs, halved
- 4 scallions, both white and green parts, thinly sliced

1. In a large skillet, heat the oil over medium-high heat. Add the beef and cook, stirring, until just cooked through, 5 minutes. Stir in the broth and curry. Add the carrots and bring to a boil. Reduce the heat to medium-low and simmer until the carrots are tender, about 5 minutes. Stir in the peas and cook just until heated through, 2 minutes more.
2. In a pot, heat the broth over medium-high heat until simmering.
3. Into each of 4 serving bowls, place 2 tablespoons of the tare. Divide the noodles among the bowls and ladle the broth over the noodles. Divide the meat and sauce, veggies, eggs, and scallions among the bowls. Serve immediately.

Ramen For Beginners | 31

Vegan Kare Shio
Prep Time: 15 minutes | Cook Time: 10 minutes | Serves 4

- ½ cup Shio Tare
- ½ cup Kare (Curry) Coconut Tare
- 4 cups Vegan Broth
- 1 ounce dried shiitake mushrooms, sliced
- 1 pound silken tofu, cut into 1-inch squares
- 16 snow or sugar snap pea pods
- 4 shishito peppers, seeded and cut into ⅛-inch circles
- ¼ cup sliced scallion, green and white parts
- 1 sheet nori, cut into 3-by-½-inch strips

1. Spoon 2 tablespoons of shio tare into each serving bowl.
2. Spoon 2 tablespoons of coconut tare into each serving bowl.
3. In a large saucepan over high heat, bring the broth and mushrooms to a simmer.
4. Remove the rehydrated mushrooms from the broth and distribute them among the bowls.
5. Bring a large stockpot full of water to a boil over high heat. Add the noodles and boil (1 minute for fresh, 3 to 4 minutes for dry), then drain.
6. Just before the noodles are done, ladle the broth into the bowls. Add the noodles to each bowl and stir gently, mixing the noodles, tare, vegetables, and broth.
7. Top each bowl with the scallion and nori strips.
8. Serve immediately.

Shiitake Shio Ramen with Crab, Corn, and Pickled Daikon Radish
Prep Time: 15 minutes | Cook Time: 20 minutes | Serves 4

- 1 tablespoon butter
- 4 ounces fresh shiitake mushrooms, sliced
- 1 garlic clove, minced
- Pinch salt
- ½ cup Shio Tare
- 8 cups Awase Dashi
- 18 ounces Basic Ramen Noodles (or store-bought) or 12 ounces dried ramen noodles
- 1 cup cooked lump Dungeness crab meat
- 1 cup fresh corn kernels (from 2 ears of corn)
- 12 slices Pickled Daikon Radish

1. In a large skillet, melt the butter over medium-high heat until it bubbles. Add the mushrooms, garlic, and salt and cook, stirring occasionally, until the mushrooms are softened, about 5 minutes.
2. Cook the noodles according to the recipe (or package instructions) and then drain well.
3. When the noodles are done cooking, immediately ladle the hot soup into the serving bowls over the tare. Add ¼ of the noodles to each bowl. Stir gently and lift with chopsticks to distribute the tare into the broth and to coat the noodles. The noodles should float on top somewhat.
4. Top each bowl with ¼ cup of the crab meat, ¼ cup of the corn, ¼ of the mushrooms, and 3 slices of the pickled daikon radish. Serve immediately.

Shio Ramen with Chashu Pork Belly, Clams and Black Truffle Oil

Prep Time: 15 minutes | Cook Time: 25 minutes | Serves 4

- 1 pound live littleneck clams, scrubbed clean
- ½ cup Shio Tare
- 8 cups Tonkotsu
- 2 tablespoons neutral-flavored vegetable oil
- 12 slices Chashu Pork Belly
- 18 ounces Basic Ramen Noodles (or store-bought) or 12 ounces dried ramen noodles
- 2 teaspoons black truffle oil
- 1 cup microgreens

1. In a medium saucepan, bring about 4 inches of water to a boil over high heat. Reduce the heat to medium, add the clams, cover, and cook for about 10 minutes, until most of the clam shells have opened (discard any that haven't opened). Use a slotted spoon to remove the clams from the pot. Set aside.
2. Spoon 2 tablespoons of the tare into each of 4 serving bowls.
3. In a large saucepan, heat the Tonkotsu over high heat until it is just about to boil.
4. While the broth is heating, heat the vegetable oil in a skillet and warm the pork slices in it for 1 to 2 minutes on each side.
5. Cook the noodles according to the recipe (or package instructions) and then drain well.
6. When the noodles are done cooking, immediately ladle the hot soup into the serving bowls over the tare. Add ¼ of the noodles to each bowl. Stir gently and lift with chopsticks to distribute the tare into the broth and to coat the noodles. The noodles should float on top somewhat.
7. Top each bowl with several clams, 3 slices of pork, ½ teaspoon of black truffle oil, and ¼ cup of the microgreens. Serve immediately.

Shio Ramen with Crispy Fried Squid, Squid Ink, and Salmon Roe

Prep Time: 15 minutes | Cook Time: 15 minutes | Serves 4

- ½ cup Shio Tare
- 8 cups Clear Chicken Broth
- 2 teaspoons squid ink
- 18 ounces Basic Ramen Noodles (or store-bought) or 12 ounces dried ramen noodles
- Crispy Fried Squid
- 2 ounces salmon roe
- 2 cups arugula

1. Spoon 2 tablespoons of the tare into each of 4 serving bowls.
2. In a large saucepan, heat the Clear Chicken Broth over high heat until it is just about to boil. Remove from the heat and immediately stir in the squid ink.
3. Cook the noodles according to the recipe (or package instructions) and then drain well.
4. When the noodles are done cooking, immediately ladle the hot soup into the serving bowls over the tare. Add ¼ of the noodles to each bowl. Stir gently and lift with chopsticks to distribute the tare into the broth and to coat the noodles. The noodles should float on top somewhat.
5. Top each bowl with ¼ of the Crispy Fried Squid, ¼ of the salmon roe, and ½ cup of the arugula. Serve immediately.

Hakodate Shio Ramen with Spicy Ground Chicken

Prep Time: 15 minutes | Cook Time: 20 minutes | Serves 4

- 1 pound ground chicken
- ½ teaspoon salt
- 1 garlic clove, minced
- 1 teaspoon soy sauce
- 1 tablespoon Chili Oil
- ½ cup Shio Tare
- 6 cups Clear Chicken Broth
- 2 cups Awase Dashi
- 18 ounces Basic Ramen Noodles (or store-bought) or 12 ounces dried ramen noodles
- ¼ cup sliced scallions, green and white parts

1. Heat a large skillet over medium-high heat. Add the chicken and salt and cook, stirring occasionally and breaking up with a spatula, until the meat is browned, about 5 minutes.
2. Add the garlic and cook, stirring, for 1 minute more. Stir in the soy sauce and remove from the heat. Stir in the Chili Oil.
3. Spoon 2 tablespoons of the tare into each of 4 serving bowls.
4. In a large saucepan, combine the Clear Chicken Broth and Awase Dashi and heat over high heat until it is just about to boil.
5. Cook the noodles according to the recipe (or package instructions) and then drain well.
6. When the noodles are done cooking, immediately ladle the hot soup into the serving bowls over the tare. Add ¼ of the noodles to each bowl. Stir gently and lift with chopsticks to distribute the tare into the broth and to coat the noodles. The noodles should float on top somewhat.
7. Top each bowl with ¼ of the chicken mixture and 1 tablespoon of the scallions and serve immediately.

Shio Ramen with Ginger Chicken, Soy Sauce Eggs, and Yuzu

Prep Time: 15 minutes plus 30 minutes to marinate | Cook Time: 20 minutes | Serves 4

- 1½ tablespoons soy sauce
- 1½ tablespoons sake
- 1½ tablespoons honey
- 1 tablespoon grated fresh ginger
- 1 pound boneless chicken thighs, cut into bite-size pieces
- 1 tablespoon neutral-flavored vegetable oil
- ½ cup Shio Tare
- 2 tablespoons yuzu juice
- 8 cups Clear Chicken Broth
- 18 ounces Basic Ramen Noodles (or store-bought) or 12 ounces dried ramen noodles
- 2 Soy Sauce Eggs, halved lengthwise
- ¼ cup sliced scallions, green and white parts

1. In a medium mixing bowl, whisk together the soy sauce, sake, honey, and ginger. Add the chicken and toss to coat well. Cover and refrigerate for 30 minutes.
2. In a large skillet, heat the vegetable oil over medium heat until it shimmers. Add the chicken and cook, stirring occasionally, until the chicken is browned on all sides, 5 to 7 minutes.
3. Add the marinade to the pan and cook, stirring, to coat the chicken. Let simmer for 1 to 2 minutes, until the sauce thickens a bit.
4. Spoon 2 tablespoons of the tare into each of 4 serving bowls. Add 1½ teaspoons of yuzu juice to each bowl.
5. In a large saucepan, heat the Clear Chicken Broth over high heat until it is just about to boil.
6. Cook the noodles according to the recipe (or package instructions) and then drain well.
7. When the noodles are done cooking, immediately ladle the hot soup into the serving bowls over the tare and yuzu juice. Add ¼ of the noodles to each bowl. Stir gently and lift with chopsticks to distribute the tare into the broth and to coat the noodles. The noodles should float on top somewhat.
8. Top each bowl with ¼ of the chicken, half of 1 egg, and 1 tablespoon of the scallions. Serve immediately.

Shiitake Shio Ramen with Silken Tofu, Mushrooms, and Crispy Shallots

Prep Time: 15 minutes | Cook Time: 20 minutes | Serves 4

- 3 tablespoons neutral-flavored vegetable oil, divided
- 4 ounces fresh shiitake mushrooms, sliced
- 1 garlic clove, minced
- Pinch salt
- 1 medium shallot, thinly sliced
- ½ cup Shio Tare
- 8 cups Shiitake Dashi
- 18 ounces Basic Ramen Noodles (or store-bought) or 12 ounces dried ramen noodles
- 6 ounces silken tofu, diced

1. In a large skillet, heat 1 tablespoon of vegetable oil over medium-high heat until it shimmers. Add the mushrooms, garlic, and salt and cook, stirring occasionally, until the mushrooms are softened, about 5 minutes.
2. In a small bowl, toss the shallot with the remaining 2 tablespoons of vegetable oil. Spread the shallot slices out into a single layer on a microwave-safe plate. Microwave in 30-second intervals, until the shallots turn golden brown, about 2 minutes total. Stop cooking when they are mostly brown, but not too dark. Keep in mind that they will continue to cook after being removed from the microwave because the oil will be very hot.
3. Spoon 2 tablespoons of the tare into each of 4 serving bowls.
4. In a large saucepan, heat the Shiitake Dashi over high heat until it is just about to boil.
5. Cook the noodles according to the recipe (or package instructions) and then drain well.
6. When the noodles are done cooking, immediately ladle the hot soup into the serving bowls over the tare. Add ¼ of the noodles to each bowl. Stir gently and lift with chopsticks to distribute the tare into the broth and to coat the noodles. The noodles should float on top somewhat.
7. Top each bowl with ¼ of the tofu, ¼ of the mushrooms, and ¼ of the shallots. Serve immediately.

Teriyaki Chicken and Salmon Shio
Prep Time: 15 minutes | Cook Time: 10 minutes | Serves 4

- 1 cup Shio Tare
- 2 cups Fish Broth
- 2 cups Clear Chicken Broth
- 1 ounce dried shiitake mushrooms, sliced
- 1 garlic clove, crushed and chopped
- 1 tablespoon (1-inch piece) fresh ginger, unpeeled, crushed and chopped
- 1 tablespoon honey
- 1 tablespoon soy sauce
- 1 tablespoon mirin
- 8 ounces boneless chicken thighs, cut into bite-size pieces
- 8 ounces salmon fillet, whole or cut into bite-size pieces
- 2 tablespoons vegetable oil, divided
- 24 snow or sugar snap pea pods
- 1 pound fresh or Homemade Ramen Noodles, or 8 ounces dried noodles
- ¼ cup sliced scallion, green and white parts
- 1 sheet nori, cut into 3-by-½-inch strips

1. Spoon ¼ cup of tare into each serving bowl.
2. In a large saucepan over high heat, bring the fish broth, chicken broth, and mushrooms to a simmer.
3. Remove the rehydrated mushrooms from the broth and divide among the bowls.
4. In a large bowl, combine the garlic, ginger, honey, soy sauce, and mirin; divide the mixture between two bowls. Add the chicken and salmon pieces in the separate bowls and marinate for 5 minutes. If using a whole piece of salmon, marinate at room temperature for 20 minutes.
5. Heat 1 tablespoon of oil in a large skillet over high heat. When it just begins to smoke, add the chicken and stir-fry for about 5 minutes, until lightly brown and crispy. Remove and set aside.
6. Add the remaining 1 tablespoon of oil to the skillet and stir-fry the salmon for about 3 minutes, until lightly brown and crispy. Remove and set aside.
7. Distribute the pea pods among the bowls.
8. Bring a large stockpot full of water to a boil over high heat. Add the noodles and boil (1 minute for fresh, 3 to 4 minutes for dry), then drain.
9. Just before the noodles are done, ladle the broth into the bowls. Add the noodles to each bowl and stir gently, mixing the noodles, pea pods, tare, and broth.
10. To each bowl, add the chicken and salmon and top with the scallion and nori strips.
11. Serve immediately.

Spring Shio Ramen with Baby Bok Choy, Peas, and Soft-Boiled Eggs
Prep Time: 15 minutes | Cook Time: 20 minutes | Serves 4

- 1 tablespoon sesame oil
- 2 garlic cloves, minced
- 2 teaspoons grated fresh ginger
- 4 scallions, sliced, green and white parts separated
- ⅓ pound baby bok choy
- 12 ounces shelled English peas
- ½ cup Shio Tare
- 4 teaspoons Scallion Oil
- 8 cups Shiitake Dashi
- 18 ounces Basic Ramen Noodles (or store-bought) or 12 ounces dried ramen noodles
- 2 Soft-Boiled Eggs, halved lengthwise
- 2 ounces pea shoots

1. In a large skillet, heat the sesame oil over medium heat until it shimmers. Add the garlic, ginger, and scallion whites. Cook, stirring frequently, until fragrant, about 1 minute. Add the baby bok choy and peas and cook, stirring occasionally, for about 2 minutes more, until wilted. Remove from the heat.
2. Spoon 2 tablespoons of the tare into each of 4 serving bowls. Add 1 teaspoon of Scallion Oil to each bowl.
3. In a large saucepan, heat the Shiitake Dashi over high heat until it is just about to boil.
4. Cook the noodles according to the recipe (or package instructions) and then drain well.
5. When the noodles are done cooking, immediately ladle the hot soup into the serving bowls over the tare and oil. Add ¼ of the noodles to each bowl. Stir gently and lift with chopsticks to distribute the tare into the broth and to coat the noodles. The noodles should float on top somewhat.
6. Top each bowl with half of 1 Soft-Boiled Egg, ¼ of the bok choy and peas mixture, ¼ of the scallion greens, and ¼ of the pea shoots. Serve immediately.

Ramen For Beginners | 35

Chapter 5
Shoyu Ramen

Traditional Shoyu Ramen
Prep Time: 10 minutes | Cook Time: 10 minutes | Serves 4

- ½ cup Shoyu Tare
- 5 cups any type clear soup (here, here, here, here)
- 1⅓ pounds fresh noodles, such as Chukasuimen
- 4 to 8 slices Chicken Chashu
- 4 large pieces nori seaweed
- 4 slices naruto (Japanese fish cake)
- 4 Ajitama, halved
- 12 to 16 pieces Menma
- Negi

1. with all your ingredients ready to go, bring a large pot of water to a boil over medium-high heat.
2. Heat your ramen bowls by filling them halfway with hot water. The bowls don't need to be scalding, but they should be hot to the touch. Dump out the hot water and dry the bowls with some paper towels or a clean towel.
3. Put the tare and soup in a medium saucepan. Mix and bring to a simmer over low heat.
4. Cook the noodles in the large pot of boiling water. Ramen that has been cut to a standard thickness (about 1 mm) will cook in 1 to 2 minutes.
5. About 30 seconds before the noodles are finished cooking, ladle the soup into the ramen bowls.
6. Drain the noodles, taking care to shake off as much excess water as you can. Carefully place some noodles in each bowl of soup, keeping them tidy.
7. Place 1 or 2 slices of chashu, 1 piece of nori, 1 slice of naruto, 1 egg, 3 or 4 pieces of menma, and a sprinkle of negi neatly on the ramen. (The sheet of nori should be placed so just the tip is in the soup, with the rest perching on the side of the bowl. The naruto fish cake should go right in the middle.) Serve immediately.

Vegan Shoyu Ramen
Prep Time: 10 minutes | Cook Time: 10 minutes | Serves 4

- 6 teaspoons garlic oil (tip)
- 6 teaspoons Negi Oil
- ½ cup Vegetarian Shoyu Tare
- 5 cups Vegetarian Clear Soup
- 1⅓ pounds fresh noodles, such as Chukasuimen
- 12 to 16 pieces Menma
- Green Vegetable Topping
- Negi

1. with all your ingredients ready to go, bring a large pot of water to a boil over medium-high heat.
2. Heat your ramen bowls by filling them halfway with hot water. The bowls don't need to be scalding, but they should be hot to the touch. Dump out the hot water and dry the bowls with some paper towels or a clean towel.
3. Put 1½ teaspoons of garlic oil and 1½ teaspoons of negi oil in each ramen bowl.
4. Put the tare and soup in a medium saucepan. Mix and bring to a simmer over low heat.
5. Cook the noodles in the large pot of boiling water. Ramen that has been cut to a standard thickness (about 1 mm) will cook in 1 to 2 minutes.
6. About 30 seconds before the noodles are finished cooking, ladle the soup into the ramen bowls.
7. Drain the noodles, taking care to shake off as much excess water as you can. Carefully place some noodles in each bowl of soup, keeping them tidy.
8. Place 3 or 4 pieces of menma, some green vegetables, and a sprinkle of negi neatly on the ramen. Serve immediately.

Shoyu Ramen with Panko-Breaded Chicken and Spinach
Prep Time: 15 minutes | Cook Time: 15 minutes | Serves 4

- 1 pound chicken breast tenders
- ½ teaspoon kosher salt
- ½ teaspoon freshly ground black pepper
- 1 cup panko bread crumbs
- 1 large egg, beaten
- 8 cups Basic Chicken Broth or store-bought broth
- ½ cup Basic Shoyu Tare
- 18 ounces fresh ramen noodles, 12 ounces dried ramen noodles, or 2 packages instant ramen noodles, cooked according to package directions
- 6 cups fresh spinach leaves, blanched in boiling water or wilted in a nonstick pan
- 4 teaspoons sesame oil

1. Preheat the oven to 375°F, line a baking sheet with parchment paper or aluminum foil, and set it aside.
2. Season the chicken pieces with the salt and pepper.
3. Put the panko in a shallow bowl and the egg in a separate shallow bowl.
4. Dunk the chicken pieces first in the egg and then in the panko, turning to make sure each piece is well coated.
5. Arrange the chicken pieces on the prepared baking sheet. Bake for 13 to 15 minutes, until golden brown, crisp on the outside, and cooked through.
6. In a pot, heat the broth over medium-high heat until simmering.
7. Into each of 4 serving bowls, put 2 tablespoons of tare. Divide the noodles among the bowls and ladle the broth over the noodles. Divide the chicken and spinach among the bowls. Drizzle 1 teaspoon of sesame oil over each bowl and serve immediately.

Shoyu Ramen with Sake-Steamed Chicken Drumsticks

Prep Time: 10 minutes plus 15 minutes to marinate | **Cook Time:** 20 minutes | **Serves** 4

- ¾ cup sake
- ¾ cup water
- 4 chicken drumsticks
- Kosher salt
- 1 tablespoon soy sauce
- 1 tablespoon freshly squeezed orange juice
- 2 teaspoons rice vinegar
- 2 teaspoons peeled, minced fresh ginger
- 1 teaspoon mirin
- 1 garlic clove, minced
- 8 cups Basic Chicken Broth or store-bought broth
- ½ cup Basic Shoyu Tare
- 18 ounces fresh ramen noodles, 12 ounces dried ramen noodles, or 2 packages instant ramen noodles, cooked according to package directions
- 3 scallions, both white and green parts, thinly sliced

1. In a stockpot or large saucepan, place a steamer basket. Put the sake and water in the pot and bring the liquid to a boil.
2. Season the drumsticks generously with salt and place them in the steamer basket. Cover the pot and reduce the heat to low. Steam the chicken for about 20 minutes, until it is cooked through.
3. In a medium bowl, combine the soy sauce, orange juice, vinegar, ginger, mirin, and garlic, and stir to mix. Add the chicken to the bowl and toss to coat. Let it stand for 15 minutes while you prepare the soup.
4. To make the soup, heat the broth over medium-high heat until simmering.
5. Into each of 4 serving bowls, put 2 tablespoons of tare. Divide the noodles among the bowls and ladle the broth over the noodles. Arrange a drumstick and scallions on top of each bowl. Serve immediately.

Shoyu Ramen with Crispy Chicken Strips

Prep Time: 10 minutes | **Cook Time:** 15 minutes | **Serves** 4

- 1 pound chicken breast tenders
- ½ teaspoon kosher salt
- ½ teaspoon freshly ground black pepper
- 1 large egg, beaten
- 1 cup panko bread crumbs
- 8 cups Basic Chicken Broth or store-bought broth
- ½ cup Basic Shoyu Tare
- 18 ounces fresh ramen noodles, 12 ounces dried ramen noodles, or 2 packages instant ramen noodles, cooked according to package directions
- 1 sheet nori, cut into 3-inch strips
- 2 Soft-Boiled Eggs, halved

1. Preheat the oven to 375°F and line a baking sheet with parchment paper or aluminum foil.
2. Season the chicken pieces with the salt and pepper.
3. Place the egg in a shallow bowl and the panko in another shallow bowl.
4. Dunk the chicken pieces first in the egg and then in the panko, turning to make sure each piece is well coated.
5. Arrange the chicken pieces on the prepared baking sheet. Bake for 13 to 15 minutes, until golden brown and crisp on the outside and cooked through.
6. To make the soup, heat the broth over medium-high heat until simmering.
7. Into each of 4 serving bowls, put 2 tablespoons of tare. Divide the noodles among the bowls and ladle the broth over the noodles. Divide the chicken and nori strips among the bowls and top each bowl with half an egg. Serve immediately.

Shoyu Ramen with Bacon, Soft-Boiled Eggs, and Crispy Kale

Prep Time: 10 minutes | **Cook Time:** 15 minutes | **Serves 4**

- 12 leaves Tuscan kale, stemmed and cut into 1-inch pieces
- 1½ tablespoons olive oil
- ¼ teaspoon kosher salt
- Freshly ground black pepper
- 8 cups Basic Pork Broth or store-bought broth
- ½ cup Basic Shoyu Tare
- 18 ounces fresh ramen noodles, 12 ounces dried ramen noodles, or 2 packages instant ramen noodles, cooked according to package directions
- 2 Soft-Boiled Eggs, halved
- 4 strips bacon, cooked until crisp

1. Preheat the oven to 400°F and line a baking sheet with aluminum foil.
2. In a mixing bowl, toss the kale with the olive oil. Spread the kale out on the prepared baking sheet in a single layer, sprinkle the salt and a bit of pepper over it, and roast in the oven for 10 to 15 minutes, until crispy.
3. In a pot, heat the broth over medium-high heat until simmering.
4. Into each of 4 serving bowls, put 2 tablespoons of tare. Divide the noodles among the bowls and ladle the broth over the noodles. Divide the kale among the bowls and place half an egg and 1 strip of bacon on top of each bowl. Serve immediately.

Shoyu Chicken Ramen with Miso-Glazed Carrots

Prep Time: 10 minutes | **Cook Time:** 10 minutes | **Serves 4**

- 2 teaspoons sesame oil
- 2 cups sliced carrots
- ½ cup water
- 2 teaspoons red miso paste
- 1 teaspoon peeled, grated fresh ginger
- Kosher salt
- 8 cups Basic Chicken Broth or store-bought chicken broth
- ½ cup Basic Shoyu Tare
- 18 ounces fresh ramen noodles, 12 ounces dried ramen noodles, or 2 packages instant ramen noodles, cooked according to package directions
- 12 ounces cooked, shredded chicken
- 2 tablespoons chopped chives

1. In a skillet, heat the sesame oil over medium-high heat. Add the carrots and cook for about 5 minutes, stirring occasionally, until they begin to soften.
2. In small bowl, whisk together the water, miso paste, and ginger until well combined. Add the mixture to the skillet with the carrots, reduce the heat to low, and simmer for about 5 minutes, until the carrots are tender and the liquid has reduced to a glaze. Season with salt.
3. To make the soup, heat the broth over medium-high heat until simmering.
4. Into each of 4 serving bowls, put 2 tablespoons of tare. Divide the noodles among the bowls and ladle the broth over the noodles. Divide the chicken, carrots, and chives on top of each bowl. Serve immediately.

Shoyu Ramen with Panfried Shrimp and Greens

Prep Time: 10 minutes | Cook Time: 10 minutes | Serves 4

- ½ cup soy sauce
- 2 tablespoons honey
- 1 tablespoon sesame oil
- 1 tablespoon cornstarch
- 1 tablespoon water
- 4 garlic cloves, minced
- 1 teaspoon chili paste
- 1 tablespoon cooking oil
- 1½ pounds shrimp, peeled and deveined
- 10 leaves chard or kale, tough center ribs removed and leaves julienned
- 8 cups Basic Fish Broth
- ½ cup Basic Shoyu Tare
- 18 ounces fresh ramen noodles, 12 ounces dried ramen noodles, or 2 packages instant ramen noodles, cooked according to package directions
- 4 scallions, both white and green parts, thinly sliced
- 4 teaspoons toasted sesame seeds

1. In a small bowl, whisk together the soy sauce, honey, sesame oil, cornstarch, water, garlic, and chili paste.
2. In a large skillet, heat the oil over medium-high heat. Add the shrimp and cook for about 3 minutes, stirring, until it is opaque and just cooked through.
3. Add the greens to the pan and cook, stirring, until the greens are wilted, about 3 minutes more.
4. Add the sauce mixture to the skillet and cook for about 2 minutes, until it bubbles and thickens.
5. In a pot, heat the broth over medium-high heat until simmering.
6. Into each of 4 serving bowls, put 2 tablespoons of tare. Divide the noodles among the bowls and ladle the broth over the noodles. Divide the shrimp and greens among the bowls. Garnish with the scallions and sesame seeds and serve immediately.

Shoyu Ramen with Pork Katsu, Spinach, and Chili Oil

Prep Time: 20 minutes | Cook Time: 25 minutes | Serves 4

- ½ cup Shoyu Tare
- 8 cups Clear Chicken Broth
- 4 cups fresh spinach
- 18 ounces Basic Ramen Noodles (or store-bought) or 12 ounces dried ramen noodles
- ½ cup Seasoned Bamboo Shoots
- ¼ cup sliced scallions, green and white parts
- 4 teaspoons Chili Oil or bottled chili oil
- 12 strips Pork Katsu
- ¼ cup katsu sauce

1. Spoon 2 tablespoons of the tare into each of 4 serving bowls.
2. In a large saucepan, heat the Clear Chicken Broth over high heat until it is just about to boil. Add the spinach to the broth and cook for 1 to 2 minutes, until just wilted. Remove the spinach from the broth using a slotted spoon or tongs and set aside.
3. Cook the noodles according to the recipe (or package instructions) and then drain well.
4. When the noodles are done cooking, immediately ladle the hot soup into the serving bowls over the tare. Add ¼ of the noodles to each bowl. Stir gently and lift with chopsticks to distribute the tare into the broth and to coat the noodles. The noodles should float on top somewhat.
5. Top each bowl with ¼ of the wilted spinach, ¼ of the Seasoned Bamboo Shoots, ¼ of the scallions, and 1 teaspoon of the Chili Oil. Place 3 pork pieces on top and drizzle the katsu sauce over the pork. Serve immediately.

Shoyu Ramen with Lemony Breaded Halibut

Prep Time: 15 minutes | Cook Time: 15 minutes | Serves 4

- 2 tablespoons mayonnaise
- 4 (5-ounce) halibut fillets
- ¾ cup panko bread crumbs
- Zest of 1 lemon
- Kosher salt
- Freshly ground pepper
- 8 cups Basic Fish Broth
- ½ cup Basic Shoyu Tare
- 18 ounces fresh ramen noodles, 12 ounces dried ramen noodles, or 2 packages instant ramen noodles, cooked according to package directions
- 2 Soy Sauce Eggs, halved
- 2 cups arugula
- 4 scallions, both white and green parts, thinly sliced
- 4 lemon wedges

1. Preheat the oven to 400°F. Line a rimmed baking sheet with aluminum foil.
2. Spread the mayonnaise on the fish fillets in a thin layer, completely coating each fillet.
3. In a shallow bowl, toss together the panko and lemon zest, and season the mixture with salt and pepper.
4. Press each fillet into the bread crumb mixture to coat completely. Arrange the coated fillets on the prepared baking sheet.
5. Bake for 15 minutes, or until the fish is cooked through and flakes easily with a fork.
6. In a pot, heat the broth over medium-high heat until simmering.
7. Into each of 4 serving bowls, put 2 tablespoons of tare. Divide the noodles among the bowls and ladle the broth over the noodles. In each bowl, arrange 1 fish fillet and half an egg on top and divide the arugula among the bowls. Garnish with the scallions and a lemon wedge and serve immediately.

Kitakata Ramen

Prep Time: 15 minutes | Cook Time: 10 minutes | Serves 4

- 1 cup Shoyu Tare
- 4 cups Tonkotsu Pork Broth
- 8 (¼-inch-thick) slices Chashu Pork
- 1 pound fresh udon noodles, or 8 ounces dried noodles
- 8 (¼-inch-thick) slices kamaboko (steamed fish cake)
- 4 ounces menma
- ¼ cup sliced scallion, green and white parts
- 1 sheet nori, cut into 3-by-½-inch strips

1. Spoon ¼ cup of tare into each serving bowl.
2. In a large saucepan over medium heat, bring the broth to a simmer.
3. In a large dry skillet over medium-high heat, sear the chashu on both sides, about 3 minutes, until light golden brown. Set aside.
4. Bring a large stockpot full of water to a boil over high heat. Add the noodles and boil (1 minute for fresh, 3 to 4 minutes for dry), then drain.
5. Just before the noodles are done, ladle the broth into the bowls. Add the noodles to each bowl and stir gently, mixing the noodles, tare, and broth.
6. Top the bowls with the chashu, kamaboko, menma, scallion, and nori strips.
7. Serve immediately.

Onomichi Ramen

Prep Time: 15 minutes | **Cook Time:** 10 minutes | **Serves 4**

- 1 cup Shoyu Tare
- 4 cups Fish Broth
- 8 (¼-inch-thick) slices Chashu Pork
- 1 pound fresh udon noodles, or 8 ounces dried noodles
- 4 (¼-inch-thick) slices kamaboko (steamed fish cake)
- 2 Ajitama Eggs, halved lengthwise
- ¼ cup sliced scallion, green and white parts
- 4 ounces menma
- 1 sheet nori, cut into 3-by-½-inch strips

1. Place ¼ cup of tare into each serving bowl.
2. In a large saucepan over medium heat, bring the broth to a simmer.
3. In a large dry skillet over medium-high heat, sear the chashu on both sides, about 3 minutes, until light golden brown. Set aside.
4. Bring a large stockpot full of water to a boil over high heat. Add the noodles and boil (1 minute for fresh, 3 to 4 minutes for dry), then drain.
5. Just before the noodles are done, ladle the broth into the bowls. Add the noodles to each bowl and stir gently, mixing the noodles, tare, and broth.
6. Top the bowls with the kamaboko, half an egg, chashu, scallion, menma, and nori strips.
7. Serve immediately.

Shoyu Ramen with Crispy Shredded Pork and Arugula

Prep Time: 15 minutes | **Cook Time:** 6 hours 10 minutes (slow cooker) or 1 hour and 10 minutes (pressure cooker) | **Serves 4**

- 1 (3½- to 4-pound) pork shoulder, cut into a few large pieces
- 1 teaspoon kosher salt
- 1 cup water
- 1 onion, diced
- ½ cup soy sauce
- ¼ cup sake
- ¼ cup brown sugar
- 6 garlic cloves, minced
- 1-inch piece fresh ginger, peeled and sliced
- 8 cups Basic Pork Broth or store-bought broth
- ½ cup Basic Shoyu Tare
- 18 ounces fresh ramen noodles, 12 ounces dried ramen noodles, or 2 packages instant ramen noodles, cooked according to package directions
- 4 cups arugula
- 2 Soft-Boiled Eggs, halved
- 4 scallions, both white and green parts, thinly sliced

1. Into a slow cooker or pressure cooker, put the pork and season the meat all over with salt.
2. In a medium bowl, stir together the water, onion, soy sauce, sake, brown sugar, garlic, and ginger. Pour the mixture over the meat.
3. If using a slow cooker, cover and cook on high for 6 hours. If using a pressure cooker, cover, turn the valve to the sealing position, and pressure cook for 1 hour. When the cooking time is up, let the pressure release naturally.
4. When the meat is cooked, it should be very tender and shred easily with a fork. Transfer the meat to a medium bowl and let it rest for 15 minutes or so before shredding it with two forks.
5. Spread the meat out on a baking sheet and cook under the broiler for 4 to 6 minutes, until it crisps up.
6. In a pot, heat the broth over medium-high heat until simmering.
7. Into each of 4 serving bowls, put 2 tablespoons of tare. Divide the noodles among the bowls and ladle the broth over the noodles. Pile some of the cooked pork, 1 cup of arugula, and half an egg on top of each bowl and top with the scallions. Serve immediately

Shoyu Shrimp Tempura Ramen

Prep Time: 15 minutes | Cook Time: 5 minutes | Serves 4

- Cooking oil, for frying
- 1 pound large shrimp (about 12 shrimp), peeled and deveined
- ½ cup cornstarch
- 1 cup all-purpose flour
- ½ teaspoon kosher salt
- 1 large egg
- ¼ cup club soda
- 8 cups Basic Fish Broth
- ½ cup Basic Shoyu Tare
- 18 ounces fresh ramen noodles, 12 ounces dried ramen noodles, or 2 packages instant ramen noodles, cooked according to package directions
- 2 Soy Sauce Eggs or Soft-Boiled Eggs, halved
- 4 scallions, both white and green parts, thinly sliced

1. Fill a deep-sided saucepan with 2 to 3 inches of oil. Heat it over medium-high heat until it shimmers.
2. In a bowl, toss the shrimp in the cornstarch to coat.
3. In a medium bowl, whisk together the flour and salt. In small bowl, whisk together the egg and club soda until frothy. Whisk the egg mixture into the flour mixture until smooth.
4. Dunk the shrimp in the batter to coat and drop them into the hot oil. Cook for about 3 minutes, until golden brown. Transfer the shrimp to a paper towel–lined plate to drain.
5. In a pot, heat the broth over medium-high heat until simmering.
6. Into each of 4 serving bowls, put 2 tablespoons of tare. Divide the noodles among the bowls and ladle the broth over the noodles. Divide the shrimp and eggs among the bowls. Garnish each bowl with scallions and serve immediately.

Shoyu Ramen with Ginger-Braised Pork and Kimchi

Prep Time: 15 minutes | Cook Time: 3 hours | Serves 4

- 1 tablespoon sesame oil
- 1 (3-inch) piece fresh ginger, sliced into thick rounds
- 2 pounds pork shoulder, cut into large cubes
- 5 tablespoons white miso
- 3 tablespoons shoyu or low-sodium soy sauce
- ½ cup mirin
- 1 cup water
- ½ cup Shoyu Tare
- ¼ cup Rendered Chicken Fat
- 8 cups Clear Chicken Broth
- 18 ounces Basic Ramen Noodles (or store-bought) or 12 ounces dried ramen noodles
- 2 Soft-Boiled Eggs, sliced in half lengthwise
- 1 cup kimchi, drained
- ¼ cup sliced scallions, green and white parts

1. In a large saucepan, heat the sesame oil over medium heat for about 1 minute. Add the ginger and cook, stirring frequently, until the ginger is golden brown, about 1 minute. Add the pork and cook, stirring occasionally, until it is lightly browned on all sides, about 8 minutes.
2. In a mixing bowl, stir together the miso, shoyu, mirin, and water and combine well.
3. Pour the miso mixture over the pork in the saucepan. Raise the heat to medium-high and bring to a boil. Reduce the heat to low, cover, and simmer for about 3 hours, or until the pork is fork-tender. Transfer the pork from the braising liquid to a bowl and shred with 2 forks. Return the shredded meat to the braising liquid.
4. Spoon 2 tablespoons of the tare and 1 tablespoon of the chicken fat into each of 4 serving bowls.
5. In a large saucepan, heat the Clear Chicken Broth over high heat until it is just about to boil.
6. Cook the noodles according to the recipe (or package instructions) and then drain well.
7. When the noodles are done cooking, immediately ladle the hot soup into the serving bowls over the tare and fat. Add ¼ of the noodles to each bowl. Stir gently and lift with chopsticks to distribute the tare into the broth and to coat the noodles. The noodles should float on top somewhat.
8. Top each bowl with about ¼ cup of shredded pork, half of 1 egg, ¼ cup of the kimchi, and 1 tablespoon of the scallions. Serve immediately.

Shoyu Ramen with Seared Steak, Scallions, and Sesame Oil

Prep Time: 15 minutes plus 30 minutes to marinate | **Cook Time:** 25 minutes | **Serves 4**

- 2 tablespoons soy sauce
- 2 tablespoons sake
- 1 tablespoon sugar
- 1 (½-pound) New York strip steak
- Pinch salt
- Freshly ground black pepper
- 1 tablespoon neutral-flavored vegetable oil
- 1 garlic clove, thinly sliced
- ½ cup Shoyu Tare
- 8 cups Clear Chicken Broth
- 18 ounces Basic Ramen Noodles (or store-bought) or 12 ounces dried ramen noodles
- ¼ cup sliced scallions, green and white parts
- 2 tablespoons sesame oil

1. In a medium bowl, stir together the soy sauce, sake, and sugar.
2. Season the steak with salt and pepper. Add the steak to the sauce and turn to coat. Marinate the steak for at least 30 minutes, or in the refrigerator for as long as overnight.
3. In a large skillet, heat the vegetable oil over medium-high heat until it shimmers. Add the garlic and cook, stirring, just until it begins to brown, about 1 minute.
4. Add the steak to the skillet and cook, turning once, to desired doneness, about 3 minutes per side for medium-rare. Pour the marinade mixture over the steak and turn the meat to coat. Remove the meat from the pan and set aside to rest for at least 10 minutes. Slice across the grain into ½-inch-thick slices.
5. Spoon 2 tablespoons of the tare into each of 4 serving bowls.
6. In a large saucepan, heat the Clear Chicken Broth over high heat until it is just about to boil.
7. Cook the noodles according to the recipe (or package instructions) and then drain well.
8. When the noodles are done cooking, immediately ladle the hot soup into the serving bowls over the tare. Add ¼ of the noodles to each bowl. Stir gently and lift with chopsticks to distribute the tare into the broth and to coat the noodles. The noodles should float on top somewhat.
9. Top each bowl with about ¼ of the steak, 1 tablespoon of scallions, and 1½ teaspoons of sesame oil. Serve immediately.

Shoyu Ramen with Chicken Katsu, Broccoli Rabe, and Scallions

Prep Time: 20 minutes | **Cook Time:** 25 minutes | **Serves 4**

- 1 large boneless, skinless chicken breast (about 1 pound)
- ¾ teaspoon salt
- ¼ teaspoon freshly ground black pepper
- Neutral-flavored vegetable oil, for deep-frying
- 1 large egg, lightly beaten 1 cup panko bread crumbs
- ½ cup Shoyu Tare
- 8 cups Clear Chicken Broth
- ¾ pound broccoli rabe
- 18 ounces Basic Ramen Noodles (or store-bought) or 12 ounces dried ramen noodles
- ¼ cup sliced scallions, green and white parts
- ¼ cup katsu sauce

1. Slice the chicken breast horizontally into two thin slices. Cut each slice into 2 equal-size pieces. Season them with the salt and pepper and set aside.
2. Fill a deep pot with about 3 inches of vegetable oil over high heat until it shimmers.
3. Put the egg and bread crumbs in separate wide, shallow bowls. Dip a chicken piece first into the egg and then into the bread crumbs, turning to coat well. Dip the coated chicken into the egg a second time, and then coat with the bread crumbs again. Repeat with all the chicken pieces.
4. Gently lower each piece of chicken into the hot oil and cook, turning once, for about 4 minutes, until golden brown on both sides. Transfer the cooked chicken pieces to a paper towel–lined plate. Let the chicken cool for at least 5 minutes and then cut each piece into strips.
5. 1.Spoon 2 tablespoons of the tare into each of 4 serving bowls.
6. In a large saucepan, heat the Clear Chicken Broth over high heat until it is just about to boil. Add the broccoli rabe and simmer for 4 minutes, or until crisp-tender. Using a slotted spoon, remove from the broth.
7. Cook the noodles according to the recipe (or package instructions) and then drain well.
8. When the noodles are done cooking, immediately ladle the hot soup into the serving bowls over the tare. Add ¼ of the noodles to each bowl. Stir gently and lift with chopsticks to distribute the tare into the broth and to coat the noodles. The noodles should float on top somewhat.
9. Top each bowl with about 1 tablespoon of the scallions and ¼ of the broccoli rabe. Place 1 chicken piece on top and drizzle the katsu sauce over the chicken. Serve immediately.

Halal Shoyu Ramen

Prep Time: 10 minutes | Cook Time: 40 minutes | Serves 2

- 2 portions ramen noodles
- 2 1/4 cups water
- 500g chicken wings
- 1 chicken breast
- 2 scallions, roughly chopped
- 3 garlic cloves
- 6 ginger slices
- 2 cups chicken stock
- 2 8-inch pieces kombu
- 2 tablespoons oil
- 1/4 cup shoyu
- 2 tablespoon mirin-style seasoning (teriyaki or sukiyaki)
- 1 garlic, minced
- 1/2-inch ginger, minced
- 1 tablespoon roasted sesame oil
- 4 chashu chicken slices
- 2 ramen eggs
- 1 bunch scallions, finely sliced

1. Add chicken wings to a hot oiled pan over medium heat and cook for 5 minutes until lightly brown.
2. Add garlic, water, ginger, chicken breast, spring onion, chicken stock and kombu. Bring to a boil, lower the heat, cover with a lid and let simmer for 20 minutes.
3. Remove chicken breast and set aside. Cover again and simmer for 1-2 hours. Skim any excess fat from the surface. Add more water if you need to cover the meat.
4. When it's cooked, adjust seasoning to taste. Strain the soup through a colander over another pot to get a clear broth.
5. Meanwhile, heat oil in a small pan over medium heat. Add garlic, ginger and cook for 1 minute. Add soy sauce and mirin-style seasoning. Bring it to a boil, and simmer for 10 minutes on low heat. Strain and set aside.
6. Cook ramen noodles and drain them.
7. Add 2-3 tablespoons tare to each bowl. Add 1 1/2-2 cups of broth, and mix well. Add noodles, then top with listed toppings.

Black-Garlic Shoyu Ramen

Prep Time: 10 minutes | Cook Time: 35 minutes | Serves 2

- 2 ramen eggs
- 1/2 lb fresh ramen noodles
- 4 oz green beans, stem removed, sliced
- 3 oz shiitake mushrooms, thinly sliced
- 2 scallions, chopped
- 2 tablespoons soy glaze
- 2 cloves black garlic, minced
- 2 tablespoons olive oil
- 1 1-inch piece ginger, minced
- 1 tablespoon sesame oil
- 1 teaspoon furikake
- 1/2 teaspoon Jacobsen sea salt
- 1/4 cup ponzu sauce

1. Add mushrooms to a hot oiled pan over medium-high heat and cook for 4-5 minutes, stirring, until browned and crispy.
2. Add sesame oil, garlic, ginger, and white part of the scallions. Cook for 1 minute, stirring occasionally, until fragrant.
3. Add soy glaze, ponzu, and 3 cups water. Let simmer for 5 minutes, stirring. Remove from heat, add salt and pepper to taste.
4. While the broth simmers, fill a bowl with ice water and set aside.
5. Bring another pot of water to boil. Add beans and cook for 3-4 minutes, until slightly softened. Transfer cooked green beans to the bowl of ice water with a slotted spoon, leaving the pot of water boiling. Let them cool completely, then drain.
6. Add noodles to the same pot of boiling water, stirring to separate. Cook for 2-3 minutes, until tender. Drain and rinse to avoid sticking.
7. Divide noodles and broth between 2 bowls. Adjust saltiness with sea salt if necessary. Top with eggs and blanched green beans. Sprinkle with chopped green parts of scallions and furikake.

Chapter 6
Miso Ramen

Traditional Miso Ramen

Prep Time: 15 minutes | Cook Time: 10 minutes | Serves 4

- 1 cup bean sprouts
- ¾ cup Basic Miso Tare
- 5 cups any type clear soup (here, here, here, here)
- 1⅓ pounds fresh noodles (⅓ pound per bowl), such as Chukasuimen
- 4 to 8 thick slices Pork Chashu
- Negi
- Grated fresh ginger

1. Bring a medium saucepan of water to a boil over medium-high heat. Blanch the bean sprouts in the boiling water for 20 seconds. Drain and set aside with the rest of the toppings.
2. with all your ingredients ready to go, bring a large pot of water to a boil over medium-high heat.
3. Heat your ramen bowls by filling them halfway with hot water. The bowls don't need to be scalding, but they should be hot to the touch. Dump out the hot water and dry the bowls with some paper towels or a clean towel.
4. Put the tare and soup in a medium saucepan. Mix and bring to a simmer over low heat.
5. Cook the noodles in the large pot of boiling water. Ramen that has been cut to a standard thickness (about 1 mm) will cook in 1 to 2 minutes.
6. About 30 seconds before the noodles are finished cooking, ladle the soup into the ramen bowls.
7. Drain the noodles, taking care to shake off as much excess water as you can. Carefully place some noodles in each bowl of soup, keeping them tidy.
8. Place ¼ cup of bean sprouts, 1 or 2 slices of chashu, a sprinkle of negi, and a sprinkle of ginger neatly on the ramen. Serve immediately.

Wakame (Seaweed) Miso Ramen

Prep Time: 10 minutes | Cook Time: 10 minutes | Serves 4

- 1 cup dried wakame seaweed
- ¾ cup Light Miso Tare with Shiro Miso
- 5 cups Vegetarian Clear Soup
- 1⅓ pounds fresh noodles, such as Chukasuimen
- Negi

1. Soak the wakame in water for about 20 minutes. Bring a medium saucepan of water to a boil over medium-high heat and blanch the wakame for 2 minutes. Remove and set aside with the rest of the toppings.
2. with all your ingredients ready to go, bring a large pot of water to a boil over medium-high heat.
3. Heat your ramen bowls by filling them halfway with hot water. The bowls don't need to be scalding, but they should be hot to the touch. Dump out the hot water and dry the bowls with some paper towels or a clean towel.
4. Put the tare and soup in a medium saucepan. Mix and bring to a simmer over low heat.
5. Cook the noodles in the large pot of boiling water. Ramen that has been cut to a standard thickness (about 1 mm) will cook in 1 to 2 minutes.
6. About 30 seconds before the noodles are finished cooking, ladle the soup into the ramen bowls.
7. Drain the noodles, taking care to shake off as much excess water as you can. Carefully place some noodles in each bowl of soup, keeping them tidy.
8. Place some wakame and a sprinkle of negi neatly on the ramen. Serve immediately.

Miso Ramen with Braised Chicken Thighs

Prep Time: 15 minutes plus 30 minutes to marinate | Cook Time: 30 minutes | Serves 4

- ¼ cup soy sauce or tamari
- 2 tablespoons mirin
- 2 teaspoons honey or brown sugar
- 1 garlic clove, chopped
- 4 boneless, skinless chicken thighs
- 1 tablespoon cooking oil
- 1 small onion, thinly sliced
- 4 ounces shiitake mushrooms, stemmed and sliced
- 2 cups water
- 6 tablespoons miso paste
- 2 tablespoons sugar
- 2 tablespoons sake
- 18 ounces fresh ramen noodles, 12 ounces dried ramen noodles, or 2 packages instant ramen noodles, cooked according to package directions
- 1 tablespoon cooking oil
- 10 leaves chard, center ribs removed, julienned
- 1 garlic clove, minced
- Salt
- Freshly ground black pepper
- 2 Soft-Boiled Eggs, halved

1. In a medium bowl, combine the soy sauce, mirin, honey, garlic, and ginger, and stir to mix. Add the chicken and toss to coat. Refrigerate for at least 30 minutes.
2. Reduce the heat to medium and add the chicken and marinade to the pot. Simmer, reducing the heat if needed, for 15 to 20 minutes, until the chicken is cooked through.
3. Using a slotted spoon, remove the chicken and transfer it to a bowl. When the chicken is cool enough to handle, slice each thigh, keeping the slices for each thigh together.
4. Stir the miso paste, sugar, and sake into the soup and simmer for about 3 minutes, stirring occasionally, until the miso paste is melted and incorporated.
5. While the soup is cooking, in a skillet heat the oil over medium heat. Add the chard and garlic. Cook for about 4 minutes, stirring, until the chard is wilted and tender. Season the chard with salt and pepper.
6. Divide the noodles among 4 serving bowls and ladle the broth over the noodles. Top each bowl with a sliced chicken thigh, some of the mushrooms, some of the chard, and half an egg. Serve hot.

Ramen For Beginners | 47

Miso Ramen with Garlic Chicken and Soy Sauce Eggs
Prep Time: 15 minutes | Cook Time: 15 minutes | Serves 4

- 2 tablespoons cornstarch
- 1 teaspoon kosher salt
- ½ teaspoon freshly ground black pepper
- 1 pound boneless, skinless chicken thighs, cut into 2-inch pieces
- 2 tablespoons cooking oil
- 4 garlic cloves, sliced
- 2 tablespoons mirin
- 2 tablespoons soy sauce
- ¼ teaspoon sugar
- 8 cups Basic Chicken Broth or store-bought broth
- 1 jalapeño, thinly sliced
- 2 Soy Sauce Eggs or Soft-Boiled Eggs, halved

1. In a medium bowl, whisk the cornstarch, salt, and pepper. Add the chicken pieces and toss to coat them well.
2. In a medium skillet, heat the oil over medium-high heat. Add the chicken pieces and garlic and cook for about 4 minutes, turning the chicken pieces occasionally, until they are golden brown and cooked through.
3. Add the mirin, soy sauce, and sugar, toss to combine, and heat through. Remove the pan from the heat.
4. In a pot, heat the broth over medium-high heat until simmering.
5. Into each of 4 serving bowls, put 2 tablespoons of tare. Divide the noodles among the bowls and ladle the broth over the noodles. Arrange some of the chicken, a few jalapeño slices, and half an egg on top of each bowl. Serve immediately.

Miso-Ginger Ramen with Chicken and Blackened Lemons
Prep Time: 15 minutes | Cook Time: 10 minutes | Serves 4

- 8 cups Basic Chicken Broth or store-bought broth
- 2 small lemons, washed well, halved, and visible seeds removed
- ½ cup Basic Miso Tare
- 2 teaspoons peeled, grated fresh ginger
- 18 ounces fresh ramen noodles, 12 ounces dried ramen noodles, or 2 packages instant ramen noodles, cooked according to package directions
- 12 ounces cooked, shredded chicken

1. In a pot, heat the broth over medium-high heat until simmering.
2. Heat a grill or skillet over high heat. Place the lemons cut-side down on the grill or skillet. Cook for 3 to 5 minutes, until the lemons are heated through and charred on the cut sides. Ideally, you'll cook them without moving them so they char nicely, but if the heat seems uneven, adjust them so they char evenly.
3. In a small bowl, stir together the miso tare and ginger.
4. Into each of 4 serving bowls, put 2 tablespoons of the tare-ginger mixture. Divide the noodles among the bowls and ladle the broth over the noodles. Arrange some of the chicken and a charred lemon half on top of each bowl. Serve immediately. Diners can squeeze the lemon into the broth for added flavor.

Miso Ramen with Crispy Pork Katsu and Black Garlic Oil
Prep Time: 15 minutes | Cook Time: 15 minutes | Serves 4

- ½ cup Miso Tare
- 4 teaspoons Black Garlic Oil
- 8 cups Clear Chicken Broth
- 18 ounces Basic Ramen Noodles (or store-bought) or 12 ounces dried ramen noodles
- Pork Katsu
- 2 Soft-Boiled Eggs, halved lengthwise

1. Spoon 2 tablespoons of the tare into each of 4 serving bowls. Add 1 teaspoon of Black Garlic Oil to each bowl.
2. Cook the noodles according to the recipe (or package instructions) and then drain well.
3. When the noodles are finished cooking, immediately ladle the hot broth into the serving bowls over the tare and oil. Add ¼ of the noodles to each bowl. Stir gently and lift with chopsticks to distribute the tare and oil into the broth and to coat the noodles. The noodles should float on top somewhat.
4. Top each bowl with ¼ of the pork and half of 1 Soft-Boiled Egg. Serve immediately.

Miso Curry Soy Milk Ramen
Prep Time: 5 minutes | Cook Time: 20 minutes | Serves 2

- 1 tablespoon white miso paste
- 2-3 cups soy milk
- 3 tablespoons curry powder
- 2 portions ramen noodles
- 1 tablespoon vegan butter
- 1 whole bamboo shoot, slice this into quarters
- 3 chashu chicken slices
- 1 wakame seaweed sheets, sliced into pieces
- 1 cup bean sprouts
- 1 tablespoon curry powder
- 1 teaspoon water

1. Add milk to a pan and heat slowly. DO NOT BOIL. Once it's warm, add miso and mix to dissolve, then add curry powder and mix well. The curry powder will thicken the milk.
2. Bring a pot of water boil. Steam bamboo shoots and bean sprouts for 2-3 minutes. Remove and cook noodles in the same pot, following the recipe or directions on the package.
3. When noodles are cooked, add a ladle of miso curry soy milk to the serving bowls, drain noodles and place them in the bowls.
4. Top with bean sprouts, bamboo shoots and a piece of butter.

Peanut Miso

Prep Time: 15 minutes | Cook Time: 10 minutes | Serves 4

- ½ cup Miso Tare
- 6 cups Vegan Broth
- 1 ounce dried shiitake mushrooms, sliced
- ¼ cup peanut butter
- 1 teaspoon spicy sesame oil
- 1 pound fresh or Homemade Ramen Noodles, or 8 ounces dried noodles
- 4 Ajitama Eggs, halved lengthwise
- ¼ cup sliced scallion, green and white parts
- ½ cup sweet corn

1. Spoon 2 tablespoons of tare into each serving bowl.
2. In a large saucepan over medium heat, bring the broth and mushrooms to a simmer.
3. Remove the rehydrated mushrooms from the broth and divide them among the bowls.
4. Stir the peanut butter and spicy sesame oil into the broth.
5. Bring a large stockpot full of water to a boil over high heat. Add the noodles and boil (1 minute for fresh, 3 to 4 minutes for dry), then drain.
6. Just before the noodles are done, ladle the broth into the bowls. Add the noodles to each bowl and stir gently, mixing the noodles, tare, and broth.
7. Float 2 egg halves in each bowl, and top with the scallion and corn.
8. Serve immediately

Spicy Miso Ramen with Grilled Pork Tenderloin

Prep Time: 15 minutes plus 8 hours to marinate | Cook Time: 15 minutes | Serves 4

- 1½ tablespoons sugar
- 1½ tablespoons miso paste (white or red)
- 1½ tablespoons soy sauce
- 1½ tablespoons mirin
- 1½ tablespoons sesame oil
- 1½ tablespoons toasted sesame seeds
- 1 tablespoon rice vinegar
- 2 garlic cloves, minced
- 1 pound pork tenderloin
- 2 teaspoons sesame oil
- 8 ounces kale leaves, center stems removed and leaves cut into ribbons
- 8 cups Basic Pork Broth or store-bought broth
- ½ cup Spicy Miso Tare
- 18 ounces fresh ramen noodles, 12 ounces dried ramen noodles, or 2 packages instant ramen noodles, cooked according to package directions
- ½ cup chopped scallions

1. In a medium bowl, combine the sugar, miso paste, soy sauce, mirin, sesame oil, sesame seeds, vinegar, and garlic. Add the pork and turn to coat. Cover and refrigerate for 8 hours or overnight.
2. Heat a grill or grill pan to medium-high heat. Grill the pork loin for 8 to 10 minutes total, turning every few minutes, until cooked through.
3. Remove the meat from the grill and let it stand for 10 minutes before slicing it thinly.
4. In a medium skillet, heat the sesame oil over medium-high heat. Add the kale and cook for 3 to 5 minutes, stirring, until tender.
5. In a pot, heat the broth over medium-high heat until simmering.
6. Into each of 4 serving bowls, put 2 tablespoons of tare. Divide the noodles among the bowls and ladle the broth over the noodles. Divide the pork slices atop the noodles. Garnish with the scallions. Serve immediately.

Sapporo Seafood Miso

Prep Time: 15 minutes | Cook Time: 10 minutes | Serves 4

- ½ cup Miso Tare
- 6 cups Tonkotsu Pork Broth
- 12 medium shrimp, shelled, deveined, and halved lengthwise
- 1 pound fresh or Homemade Ramen Noodles, or 8 ounces dried noodles
- 4 tablespoons (½ stick) butter
- ¼ cup sliced scallion, green and white parts
- ½ cup bean sprouts
- ½ cup sweet corn
- 4 Ajitama Eggs, halved lengthwise
- 1 sheet nori, cut into 3-by-½-inch strips

1. Spoon 2 tablespoons of tare into each serving bowl.
2. In a large saucepan over medium heat, bring the broth to a simmer.
3. Add the shrimp to the broth and cook until they curl and turn opaque, about 2 minutes. Remove the shrimp and set aside.
4. Bring a large stockpot full of water to a boil over high heat. Add the noodles and boil (1 minute for fresh, 3 to 4 minutes for dry), then drain.
5. Just before the noodles are done, ladle the broth into the bowls. Add the noodles to each bowl and stir gently, mixing the tare and broth.
6. Place 1 tablespoon of butter on top of the noodles in each bowl.
7. Top the bowls with the shrimp, scallion, bean sprouts, and corn. Float 2 egg halves in each bowl, and top with the nori strips.
8. Serve immediately

Spicy Miso Ramen with Crispy Fried Chicken

Prep Time: 15 minutes plus 30 minutes to marinate | **Cook Time:** 10 minutes | **Serves 4**

- 2 tablespoons soy sauce
- 2 tablespoons sake or mirin
- 1 teaspoon sesame oil
- 1 teaspoon peeled, minced fresh ginger
- 1 teaspoon sugar
- ¼ teaspoon kosher salt
- ½ teaspoon freshly ground black pepper
- 1 pound boneless, skinless chicken thighs, cut into 2-inch pieces
- 2 teaspoons sesame oil
- 8 ounces kale leaves, center stems removed and leaves cut into ribbons
- ½ cup Spicy Miso Tare
- 18 ounces fresh ramen noodles, 12 ounces dried ramen noodles, or 2 packages instant ramen noodles, cooked according to package directions

1. In a medium bowl, stir together the soy sauce, sake, sesame oil, ginger, sugar, salt, and pepper. Add the chicken and stir to coat well. Refrigerate for at least 30 minutes.
2. Fill a saucepan with 2 to 3 inches of oil and heat it over high heat until you can see it shimmering.
3. Remove the chicken pieces from the marinade and discard the marinade.
4. In a bowl, dredge the chicken pieces in the potato starch until they are well coated.
5. Drop the chicken pieces into the hot oil and cook, turning once or twice, until they are golden brown, 3 minutes. Remove the chicken using a slotted spoon and drain it on paper towels.
6. In a pot, heat the broth over medium-high heat until simmering.
7. While the broth is heating, in a skillet, heat the sesame oil and sauté the kale for about 3 minutes, until it is softened.
8. Into each of 4 serving bowls, put 2 tablespoons of tare. Divide the noodles among the bowls and ladle the broth over the noodles. Arrange the kale and chicken on top. Serve immediately.

Miso Pumpkin Ramen with Pan-Fried Tofu and Bok Choy

Prep Time: 15 minutes | **Cook Time:** 1 hour | **Serves 4**

- 4 cups Shiitake Dashi
- ¾ cup firm tofu, cut into small rectangles
- Kosher salt
- 12 ounces Basic Ramen Noodles (or store-bought) or 5 ounces dried ramen noodles
- ⅓ pound baby bok choy
- ½ cup white miso
- 2 tablespoons shoyu
- 1 scallion, chopped, green and white parts
- ½ cup fresh corn kernels, cut from an ear of corn
- Roasted Kabocha Squash
- 1 tablespoon toasted sesame seeds

1. In a stockpot, combine the Shiitake Dashi, ginger, and garlic and bring to a boil over high heat. Immediately lower the heat to medium-low and simmer for 30 minutes.
2. In a medium nonstick skillet, heat the vegetable oil over medium-high heat until it shimmers. Add the tofu, seasoning liberally with salt, and cook, stirring frequently, until browned, about 5 minutes.
3. Cook the noodles according to the package or recipe directions and then drain.
4. Remove the broth mixture from the heat and stir in the bok choy, miso, shoyu, and scallions.
5. Ladle the broth into serving bowls. Add ¼ of the noodles to each bowl. Stir gently and lift with chopsticks to coat the noodles. The noodles should float on top somewhat.
6. Top with equal portions of tofu, bok choy, corn, kabocha squash, and sesame seeds.

Creamy Miso Chicken Ramen with Chashu Pork Belly and Maitake Mushrooms

Prep Time: 15 minutes | **Cook Time:** 30 minutes | **Serves 4**

- 8 ounces maitake mushrooms, split into small clumps
- 2 tablespoons extra-virgin olive oil
- Kosher salt
- Freshly ground black pepper
- ½ cup Miso Tare
- 8 cups "Creamy" Chicken Broth
- 1 tablespoon neutral-flavored vegetable oil
- 12 slices Chashu Pork Belly
- 18 ounces Basic Ramen Noodles (or store-bought) or 12 ounces dried ramen noodles
- 2 Soft-Boiled Eggs, halved lengthwise

1. Preheat the oven to 400°F.
2. Spoon 2 tablespoons of the tare into each of 4 serving bowls.
3. In a large saucepan, heat the "Creamy" Chicken Broth over high heat until you see bubbles around the edges and it is just about to boil.
4. While the broth is heating, heat the vegetable oil in a skillet and warm the pork slices in it for 1 to 2 minutes on each side.
5. Cook the noodles according to the recipe (or package instructions) and then drain well.
6. When the noodles are finished cooking, immediately ladle the hot broth into the serving bowls over the tare. Add ¼ of the noodles to each bowl. Stir gently and lift with chopsticks to distribute the tare into the broth and to coat the noodles. The noodles should float on top somewhat.
7. Top each bowl with 3 slices of the pork, half of 1 Soft-Boiled Egg, and ¼ of the mushrooms. Serve immediately.

Chapter 7
Tonkotsu Ramen

Traditional Tonkotsu Ramen
Prep Time: 10 minutes | Cook Time: 10 minutes | Serves 4

- ½ cup Shio Tare
- 5 cups Tonkotsu Creamy Soup
- 1⅓ pounds fresh noodles, such as thin Chukasuimen
- 4 to 8 slices Pork Chashu
- Kikurage
- Negi
- White sesame seeds
- Benishoga (red pickled ginger)
- Takana (spicy mustard greens)

1. with all your ingredients ready to go, bring a large pot of water to a boil over medium-high heat.
2. Heat your ramen bowls by filling them halfway with hot water. The bowls don't need to be scalding, but they should be hot to the touch. Dump out the hot water and dry the bowls with some paper towels or a clean towel.
3. Put the tare and soup in a medium saucepan. Mix and bring to a simmer over low heat.
4. Cook the noodles in the large pot of boiling water. Ramen that has been cut to a standard thickness (about 1 mm) will cook in 1 to 2 minutes.
5. About 30 seconds before the noodles are finished cooking, ladle the soup into the ramen bowls.
6. Drain the noodles, taking care to shake off as much excess water as you can. Carefully place some noodles in each bowl of soup, keeping them tidy.
7. Place 1 or 2 slices of chashu and a sprinkle each of kikurage and negi neatly on the ramen. Serve immediately with sesame seeds, benishoga, and takana on the side as condiments.

Negi-Baka Tonkotsu Ramen
Prep Time: 10 minutes | Cook Time: 10 minutes | Serves 4

- ½ cup Shoyu Tare
- 5 cups Tonkotsu Creamy Soup
- 1⅓ pounds fresh noodles, such as thin Chukasuimen
- 4 to 8 slices Pork Chashu
- 4 cups chopped Negi

1. with all your ingredients ready to go, bring a large pot of water to a boil over medium-high heat.
2. Heat your ramen bowls by filling them halfway with hot water. The bowls don't need to be scalding, but they should be hot to the touch. Dump out the hot water and dry the bowls with some paper towels or a clean towel.
3. Put the tare and soup in a medium saucepan. Mix and bring to a simmer over low heat.
4. Cook the noodles in the large pot of boiling water. Ramen that has been cut to a standard thickness (about 1 mm) will cook in 1 to 2 minutes.
5. About 30 seconds before the noodles are finished cooking, ladle the soup into the ramen bowls.
6. Drain the noodles, taking care to shake off as much excess water as you can. Carefully place some noodles in each bowl of soup, keeping them tidy.
7. Place 1 or 2 slices of chashu and 1 cup of negi neatly on the ramen. The scallions should cover the entire bowl. Serve immediately.

Hakata Ramen
Prep Time: 15 minutes | Cook Time: 10 minutes | Serves 4

- 1 cup Shio Tare
- 4 cups Tonkotsu Pork Broth
- 1 tablespoon miso of your choice
- 1 ounce dried shiitake mushrooms, sliced
- 8 (¼-inch-thick) slices Chashu Pork
- 1 pound fresh or Homemade Ramen Noodles, or 8 ounces dried noodles
- ½ cup sliced scallion, green and white parts
- 4 ounces pickled ginger
- 4 garlic cloves, smashed and chopped
- 4 teaspoons sesame seeds

1. Spoon ¼ cup of tare into each serving bowl.
2. In a large saucepan over medium heat, bring the broth, miso, and mushrooms to a simmer.
3. Remove the rehydrated mushrooms from the broth and divide among the bowls.
4. In a large dry skillet over medium-high heat, sear the chashu on both sides, about 3 minutes, until light golden brown. Set aside.
5. Bring a large stockpot full of water to a boil over high heat. Add the noodles and boil (1 minute for fresh, 3 to 4 minutes for dry), then drain.
6. Just before the noodles are done, ladle the broth into the bowls. Add the noodles to each bowl and stir gently, mixing the noodles, tare, mushrooms, and broth.
7. Top each bowl with the chashu, scallion, pickled ginger, garlic, and 1 teaspoon of sesame seeds.
8. Serve immediately.

Shoyu Tonkotsu with Shrimp and Mushrooms
Prep Time: 15 minutes | Cook Time: 18 minutes | Serves 4

- ½ cup Shoyu Tare
- 8 cups Tonkotsu
- ½ pound shrimp, peeled and deveined
- ½ pound button mushrooms, halved
- 2 tablespoons chili paste (sambal oelek)
- 2 teaspoons sesame oil
- 18 ounces Basic Ramen Noodles (or store-bought) or 12 ounces dried ramen noodles
- 2 Soft-Boiled Eggs, halved lengthwise
- ¼ cup sliced scallions, green and white parts
- 1 cup bean sprouts

1. Spoon 2 tablespoons of the tare into each of 4 serving bowls.
2. In a large saucepan, heat the Tonkotsu over high heat until you see bubbles around the edges and it is just about to boil. Add the shrimp and mushrooms and continue to simmer for 2 to 3 more minutes, until the shrimp are cooked through. Stir in the chili paste and sesame oil.
3. Cook the noodles according to the recipe (or package instructions) and then drain well.
4. When the noodles are done cooking, immediately ladle the hot broth into the serving bowls over the tare. Leave the shrimp and mushrooms in the pot. Add ¼ of the noodles to each bowl. Stir gently and lift with chopsticks to distribute the tare into the broth and to coat the noodles. The noodles should float on top somewhat.
5. Divide the shrimp and mushrooms among the bowls.
6. Top each bowl with half of 1 egg, 1 tablespoon of scallions, and ¼ cup of bean sprouts.

Wakayama Ramen
Prep Time: 15 minutes | Cook Time: 10 minutes | Serves 4

- 1 cup Shoyu Tare
- 4 cups Tonkotsu Pork Broth
- 8 (¼-inch-thick) slices Chashu Pork
- 1 pound fresh or Homemade Ramen Noodles, or 8 ounces dried noodles
- 2 Ajitama Eggs, halved lengthwise
- 4 (¼-inch-thick) slices kamaboko (steamed fish cake)
- ½ cup sliced scallions, green and white parts
- 4 ounces menma

1. Spoon ¼ cup of tare into each serving bowl.
2. In a large saucepan over medium heat, bring the broth to a simmer.
3. In a large dry skillet over medium-high heat, sear the chashu on both sides, about 3 minutes, until light golden brown. Set aside
4. Bring a large stockpot full of water to a boil over high heat. Add the noodles and boil (1 minute for fresh, 3 to 4 minutes for dry), then drain.
5. Just before the noodles are done, ladle the broth into the bowls. Add the noodles to each bowl and stir gently, mixing the noodles, tare, and broth.
6. Top each bowl with the chashu, half an egg, kamaboko, scallion, and menma.
7. Serve immediately.

Classic Tonkotsu Ramen with Chashu Pork and Soy Sauce Eggs
Prep Time: 15 minutes | Cook Time: 15 minutes | Serves 4

- ½ cup Shio Tare
- 8 cups Tonkotsu
- 1 teaspoon soy sauce
- Pinch kosher salt
- 1 tablespoon neutral-flavored vegetable oil
- 12 slices Chashu Pork Belly
- 18 ounces Basic Ramen Noodles (or store-bought) or 12 ounces dried ramen noodles
- 2 Soy Sauce Eggs or Soft-Boiled Eggs, sliced in half lengthwise
- ¼ cup sliced scallions, green and white parts
- 2 tablespoons Black Garlic Oil
- ¼ cup Red Pickled Ginger

1. Spoon 2 tablespoons of the tare into each of 4 serving bowls.
2. In a large saucepan, heat the Tonkotsu over high heat until you see bubbles around the edges and it is just about to boil. Stir in the soy sauce and salt.
3. While the broth is heating, heat the vegetable oil in a skillet and warm the pork slices in it for 1 to 2 minutes on each side.
4. Cook the noodles according to the recipe (or package instructions) and then drain well.
5. When the noodles are finished cooking, immediately ladle the hot broth into the serving bowls over the tare. Add ¼ of the noodles to each bowl. Stir gently and lift with chopsticks to distribute the tare into the broth and to coat the noodles. The noodles should float on top somewhat.
6. Top each bowl with 3 slices of pork, half of 1 egg, 1 tablespoon of scallions, ½ tablespoon of Black Garlic Oil, and 1 tablespoon of Red Pickled Ginger. Serve immediately.

Hakata-Style Mountain Of Scallions Ramen

Prep Time: 15 minutes | Cook Time: 15 minutes | Serves 4

- ½ cup Shio Tare
- 8 cups Tonkotsu
- 1 teaspoon soy sauce
- Pinch kosher salt
- 1 tablespoon neutral-flavored vegetable oil
- 12 slices Chashu Pork Belly
- 18 ounces Basic Ramen Noodles (or store-bought) or 12 ounces dried ramen noodles
- 2 cups sliced scallions, green and white parts

1. Spoon 2 tablespoons of the tare into each of 4 serving bowls.
2. In a large saucepan, heat the Tonkotsu over high heat until you see bubbles around the edges and it is just about to boil. Stir in the soy sauce and salt.
3. While the broth is heating, heat the vegetable oil in a skillet and warm the pork slices in it for 1 to 2 minutes on each side.
4. Cook the noodles according to the recipe (or package instructions) and then drain well.
5. When the noodles are finished cooking, immediately ladle the hot broth into the serving bowls over the tare. Add ¼ of the noodles to each bowl. Stir gently and lift with chopsticks to distribute the tare into the broth and to coat the noodles. The noodles should float on top somewhat.
6. Top each bowl with 3 slices of pork and ½ cup of the scallions. Serve immediately.

Tonkotsu Shio Ramen

Prep Time: 35 minutes | Cook Time: 16 hours | Serves 6

- 10 oz ramen noodles
- 4 lbs pork feet, cut to expose bone marrow
- 6 ramen eggs
- 12 chashu pork slices
- 1 cup sweet corn
- 1 bunch chopped green onion
- For the Shio tare:
- 2 tablespoons sea salt
- 2 tablespoons sake
- 1 tablespoon mirin
- 2 teaspoons sesame oil
- 1 teaspoon soy sauce
- 1 garlic clove, crushed

1. Place pork feet in a big stock pot and cover with water (1-2 inches above the bones). Boil for 15 min, stirring. Remove all the junk from the surface.
2. Remove from heat and strain the bones. Clean coagulated blood or dark marrow with the end of chopstick or tooth brush.
3. Return bones to the pot and cover with water a few inches above them. Bring to a rolling boil, lower the heat and simmer for 16 hours.
4. Mix together all tare ingredients and add a spoonful to the bottom of each serving bowl. Add the broth and season with more tare if needed.
5. Boil noodles according to the directions on a package and drain them.
6. Divide noodles between bowls, top with sliced pork, ramen egg, sweet corn, and chopped green onion.

Spicy Tonkotsu Ramen with Grilled Pork Tenderloin, Peanuts, and Cilantro

Prep Time: 15 minutes plus 4 hours to marinate | Cook Time: 15 minutes | Serves 4

- 3 tablespoons mirin
- 2 tablespoons soy sauce
- 2 tablespoons sesame oil
- 1 tablespoon shichimi togarashi
- 1 garlic clove, minced
- 1 pork tenderloin (about 1 pound)
- ½ cup Shoyu Tare
- 8 cups Tonkotsu
- 1 teaspoon soy sauce
- Pinch kosher salt
- 18 ounces Basic Ramen Noodles (or store-bought) or 12 ounces dried ramen noodles
- ¼ cup chopped roasted, unsalted peanuts
- ¼ cup chopped cilantro
- Shichimi togarashi, for garnish

1. In a medium bowl or resealable plastic bag, combine the mirin, soy sauce, sesame oil, shichimi togarashi, and garlic. Add the pork tenderloin and turn to coat well. Marinate for at least 4 hours, or as long as overnight.
2. Heat a grill or grill pan to medium heat. Grill the pork for 10 to 15 minutes, turning frequently, until the meat is cooked through (145°F on an instant-read meat thermometer).
3. Remove the tenderloin from the grill and let rest for 10 minutes before slicing thinly.
4. Spoon 2 tablespoons of the tare into each of 4 serving bowls.
5. In a large saucepan, heat the Tonkotsu over high heat until you see bubbles around the edges and it is just about to boil. Stir in the soy sauce and salt.
6. Cook the noodles according to the recipe (or package instructions) and then drain well.
7. When the noodles are finished cooking, immediately ladle the hot broth into the serving bowls over the tare. Add ¼ of the noodles to each bowl. Stir gently and lift with chopsticks to distribute the tare into the broth and to coat the noodles. The noodles should float on top somewhat.
8. Top each bowl with 3 slices of the pork, 1 tablespoon of the peanuts, and 1 tablespoon of the cilantro. Top with a sprinkle of shichimi togarashi. Serve immediately.

Creamy Tonkotsu Ramen
Prep Time: 25 minutes | Cook Time: 12 hours | Serves 6

- 1 large onion, skin on, chopped
- 1 3-inch knob ginger, chopped
- 2 whole leeks, washed and chopped
- 2 dozen scallions, chopped
- 6 halved ramen eggs
- 2 tablespoons vegetable oil
- 12 garlic cloves
- 6 oz enoki mushrooms
- 1 lb slab pork fatback
- 2 lbs chicken carcasses and backs, skin and fat removed
- 3 lbs pig trotters, cut crosswise into 1-inch disks

1. Heat oil in a nonstick skillet over high heat. Add garlic, onions, and ginger. Cook for 15 minutes, tossing occasionally. Set aside.
2. Add chicken and pork bones to a large stockpot and cover with cold water. Bring to a boil over high heat, then remove from heat and discard water.
3. Wash all bones under cold water, removing coagulated blood or any bits of dark marrow. Bones should become uniform grey or white after scrubbing.
4. Return bones to pot with pork fatback, scallion whites, charred vegetables, leeks, and mushrooms. Cover with cold water. Bring to a rolling boil over high heat, skimming off any scum. Wipe any scum off from around the rim of the pot with paper towel. Switch heat to low, let simmer, and place a heavy lid on top.
5. Check the broth after 15 minutes. If it's not a slow rolling boil, increase or decrease heat to adjust boiling speed. Boil for 4 hours, until fatback is fully tender.
6. Remove pork fat with a slotted spatula and place in a sealed container in the fridge.
7. Cover the pot and cook for 6-8 hours, until broth is opaque with the texture of light cream, adding more water to keep bones covered.
8. When broth is ready, turn to high heat and cook until reduced to 3 quarts. Strain into a clean pot. Repeat if you want cleaner broth. Discard any solids and fat with a ladle. Roughly chop pork fatback and whisk into broth.
9. To serve, season soup with condiments of choice and serve with cooked ramen noodles and preferable toppings.

Mayu Tonkotsu Ramen
Prep Time: 10 minutes | Cook Time: 10 minutes | Serves 4

- ½ cup Shoyu Tare
- 5 cups Tonkotsu Creamy Soup
- 1⅓ pounds fresh noodles, such as thin Chukasuimen
- 4 tablespoons garlic chips
- Negi
- 4 tablespoons Mayu

1. with all your ingredients ready to go, bring a large pot of water to a boil over medium-high heat.
2. Heat your ramen bowls by filling them halfway with hot water. The bowls don't need to be scalding, but they should be hot to the touch. Dump out the hot water and dry the bowls with some paper towels or a clean towel.
3. Put the tare and soup in a medium saucepan. Mix and bring to a simmer over low heat.
4. Cook the noodles in the large pot of boiling water. Ramen that has been cut to a standard thickness (about 1 mm) will cook in 1 to 2 minutes.
5. About 30 seconds before the noodles are finished cooking, ladle the soup into the ramen bowls.
6. Drain the noodles, taking care to shake off as much excess water as you can. Carefully place some noodles in each bowl of soup, keeping them tidy.
7. Place 1 or 2 slices of chashu, 1 tablespoon of garlic chips, and a sprinkle of negi neatly on the ramen. Drizzle 1 tablespoon of mayu over each bowl. Serve immediately.

Spicy Miso Tonkotsu Ramen with Ginger Pork
Prep Time: 15 minutes | Cook Time: 15 minutes | Serves 4

- ½ cup Spicy Miso Tare
- 8 cups Tonkotsu
- 18 ounces Basic Ramen Noodles (or store-bought) or 12 ounces dried ramen noodles
- Ginger Pork
- 2 Soft-Boiled Eggs, halved lengthwise
- ¼ cup sliced scallions, green and white parts

1. Spoon 2 tablespoons of the tare into each of 4 serving bowls.
2. In a large saucepan, heat the Tonkotsu over high heat until you see bubbles around the edges and it is just about to boil.
3. Cook the noodles according to the recipe (or package instructions) and then drain well.
4. When the noodles are done cooking, immediately ladle the hot soup into the serving bowls over the tare. Add ¼ of the noodles to each bowl. Stir gently and lift with chopsticks to distribute the tare into the broth and to coat the noodles. The noodles should float on top somewhat.
5. Top each bowl with ¼ of the Ginger Pork, half of 1 egg, and 1 tablespoon of the scallions. Serve immediately.

Chapter 8
Other Ramen

Hiyashi Chuka (Cold Chinese-Style Noodles)

Prep Time: 30 minutes | Cook Time: 10 minutes | Serves 4

- 8 large eggs
- Vegetable oil, for frying
- 1⅓ pounds fresh noodles, such as Chukasuimen
- 5 cups Light Vegetarian Soup, chilled
- 4 cups sliced ham (about 20 ounces)
- 8 Japanese or Persian cucumbers, sliced
- 4 tomatoes, cut into wedges

1. In a large bowl, beat the eggs until well combined.
2. Coat the bottom of a large skillet lightly with oil and heat over medium heat. Pour in the eggs to make one large, thin omelet. When the eggs are firm, transfer to a cutting board. Cut the omelet into thin strips and set aside to be used as a topping.
3. Bring a large pot of water to a boil over medium-high heat. Cook the noodles. Ramen that has been cut to a standard thickness (about 1 mm) will cook in 1 to 2 minutes.
4. Strain the noodles and run under cool water until the noodles are at room temperature.
5. Carefully place the noodles in your ramen bowls, keeping them tidy. Pour the cold soup over the noodles.
6. Top with the egg strips, ham and cucumber slices, and tomato wedges.

Vegan Hiyashi Chuka (Cold Chinese Noodles)

Prep Time: 10 minutes | Cook Time: 10 minutes | Serves 4

- 1⅓ pounds fresh noodles, such as Chukasuimen
- 5 cups Light Vegetarian Soup, chilled
- 4 cups chopped cooked leafy green vegetables, chilled

1. Bring a large pot of water to a boil over medium-high heat. Cook the noodles. Ramen that has been cut to a standard thickness (about 1 mm) will cook in 1 to 2 minutes.
2. Strain the noodles and run under cool water until the noodles are at room temperature.
3. Carefully place the noodles in your ramen bowls, keeping them tidy. Pour the cold soup over the noodles.
4. Top with the vegetables. Serve immediately

Morioka-Style Cold Ramen

Prep Time: 10 minutes | Cook Time: 15 minutes | Serves 4

- 5 cups Light Vegetarian Soup
- ½ cup Shoyu Tare
- 12 ice cubes
- 1⅓ pounds fresh noodles, such as Chukasuimen
- 8 slices Chicken Chashu
- 12 to 20 pieces Menma
- Negi
- 4 sheets yakinori (roasted nori)

1. In a large mixing bowl, mix the soup, tare, and ice cubes. Leave the soup in the refrigerator while you prepare the noodles.
2. Bring a large pot of water to a boil over medium-high heat. Cook the noodles. Ramen that has been cut to a standard thickness (about 1 mm) will cook in 1 to 2 minutes.
3. Strain the noodles and run under cool water until the noodles are at room temperature.
4. Carefully place the noodles in your ramen bowls, keeping them tidy. Pour the cold soup over the noodles.
5. Top with 2 slices of chashu, 3 to 5 pieces of menma, a sprinkle of negi, and a sheet of nori. Serve immediately.

Yakisoba-Style Ramen with Garlic, Chili, and Sesame Oil

Prep Time: 10 minutes | Cook Time: 10 minutes | Serves 4

- 2 tablespoons cooking oil
- 1 (14-ounce) package firm tofu, pressed and cut into chunks
- 2 garlic cloves, minced
- ⅓ cup soy sauce
- 2 teaspoons brown sugar
- 1 to 2 tablespoons chili paste
- 18 ounces fresh ramen noodles, 12 ounces dried noodles, or 2 packages instant ramen noodles, cooked al dente (1 minute less than the package directions for fresh ramen, 2 minutes less for dried ramen, and 30 seconds less for instant ramen)
- 2 scallions, both white and green parts, thinly sliced
- 1 tablespoon toasted sesame seeds
- 2 teaspoons sesame oil

1. In a large skillet, heat the oil over medium heat. Add the tofu and cook for about 5 minutes, stirring occasionally, until the tofu begins to brown. Add the garlic and cook, stirring, for 20 seconds more, until fragrant.
2. Stir in the soy sauce, brown sugar, and chili paste, and then immediately add the noodles. Toss the noodles in the sauce until they are well coated and remove the skillet from the heat.
3. Serve hot, garnished with the scallions, sesame seeds, and sesame oil.

Yamagata Cold Ramen

Prep Time: 15 minutes | Cook Time: 10 minutes | Serves 4

- 1 pound fresh or Homemade Ramen Noodles, or 8 ounces dried noodles
- 2 large eggs
- 1 tablespoon vegetable oil
- 4 pieces imitation crab legs (surimi), cut into strips
- 8 ounces sliced deli ham, cut into strips
- 1 medium carrot, julienned
- 1 medium cucumber, julienned
- 1 cup bean sprouts
- ½ cup sliced scallion, green and white parts
- 4 tablespoons sesame seeds
- 4 cups Vegan Broth, refrigerated
- ½ cup Shoyu Tare, refrigerated

1. In a bowl large enough to accommodate the cooked noodles, prepare an ice water bath.
2. Bring a large stockpot full of water to a boil over high heat. Add the noodles and boil (1 minute for fresh, 3 to 4 minutes for dry), then drain.
3. Submerge the cooked noodles in the ice water to cool them off, then drain well.
4. In a small bowl, whisk the eggs.
5. In a large skillet over medium heat, heat the oil and make a thin omelet with the eggs. Cook until set, about 3 minutes. Remove from the heat and cut into thin strips. Set aside.
6. Place a quarter of the cold noodles in each of the serving bowls.
7. Arrange the strips of egg, the crab legs, ham, carrot, and cucumber in the bowls in a circular pattern like the spokes of a wheel meeting in the center, with one ingredient making up each spoke.
8. Sprinkle the bean sprouts and scallions into the center of the bowl. Garnish with the sesame seeds.
9. In a medium bowl, whisk together the broth and the tare and divide among the bowls.
10. Serve immediately.

Tantanmen

Prep Time: 15 minutes | Cook Time: 10 minutes | Serves 4

- 4 cups Cloudy Chicken Broth
- ½ cup Shoyu Tare
- 1 tablespoon dried red chili flakes
- 1 pound ground pork
- ¼ cup Mayu
- 2 tablespoons soy sauce
- 2 tablespoons mirin
- 1 tablespoon spicy sesame oil
- 1 tablespoon (1-inch piece) fresh ginger, unpeeled, smashed, and chopped
- ¼ cup tahini
- 1 pound fresh or Homemade Ramen Noodles, or 8 ounces dried noodles
- 4 baby bok choy, stalks trimmed and separated
- ½ cup sliced scallion, green and white parts
- 2 Ajitama Eggs, halved lengthwise
- 1 cup bean sprouts
- 4 tablespoons sesame seeds

1. In a large saucepan over high heat, bring the broth, tare, and chili flakes to a boil.
2. Meanwhile, in a large skillet over medium-high heat, stir-fry the ground pork, mayu, soy sauce, mirin, oil, ginger, and tahini until the pork is cooked through, about 5 minutes. Set aside.
3. Add the noodles to the boiling broth and cook (1 minute for fresh, 3 to 4 minutes for dry).
4. Place 1 bok choy in the bottom of each serving bowl.
5. Add the noodles and broth to the bowls. Then top with the pork mixture, scallion, half an egg, bean sprouts, and sesame seeds.
6. Serve immediately.

Laksa-Style Ramen with Soft-Boiled Eggs, Green Beans, and Bean Sprouts

Prep Time: 10 minutes | Cook Time: 15 minutes | Serves 4

- 1 tablespoon cooking oil
- 2 tablespoons peeled, minced fresh ginger
- 3 garlic cloves, minced
- 1 cup laksa paste
- 1 lemongrass stalk, very thinly sliced
- 6 cups Basic Chicken Broth or water
- 2 (13.5-ounce) cans coconut milk
- 8 ounces green beans, cut into 2-inch pieces
- 1 tablespoon fish sauce
- Juice of 1 lime
- 18 ounces fresh ramen noodles, 12 ounces dried ramen noodles, or 2 packages instant ramen noodles, cooked according to package directions
- 4 Soft-Boiled Eggs, halved
- 1 cup bean sprouts
- ¼ cup chopped fresh cilantro

1. In a medium saucepan, heat the oil over medium heat. Add the ginger and garlic and cook, stirring, for about 30 seconds. Add the laksa paste and lemongrass and cook, stirring, for 2 to 3 minutes.
2. Add the broth and coconut milk and bring the mixture to a simmer. Cover and let simmer for about 5 minutes.
3. Add the green beans and fish sauce, cover again, and simmer for about 5 minutes more, until the green beans are tender.
4. Just before serving, stir in the lime juice.
5. Divide the noodles evenly between 4 serving bowls. Ladle the laksa broth and green beans over the noodles. Top each bowl with 2 egg halves and some bean sprouts. Garnish with the cilantro and serve immediately.

Tsukemen
Prep Time: 15 minutes | Cook Time: 10 minutes | Serves 4

- 3 cups Tonkotsu Pork Broth
- ½ cup Shoyu Tare
- ½ cup Miso Tare
- 1 dozen medium shrimp, peeled, deveined, and halved lengthwise
- 4 (¼-inch-thick) slices kamaboko (steamed fish cake)
- 2 Ajitama Eggs, halved lengthwise
- ½ cup sliced scallion, green and white parts
- 1 sheet nori, cut into 3-by-½-inch strips
- 1 cup bean sprouts
- 1 pound fresh udon noodles, or 8 ounces dried noodles

1. In a saucepan over high heat, bring the broth, shoyu tare, and miso tare to a simmer.
2. Poach the shrimp in the broth-tare mixture until they curl, about 2 minutes. Once poached, turn off the heat, remove the shrimp from the broth, rinse in ice water, and place in a bowl, along with the kamaboko, eggs, scallion, nori strips, and bean sprouts.
3. In a large bowl, prepare an ice water bath.
4. Bring a large stockpot full of water to a boil over high heat. Add the noodles and boil (1 minute for fresh, 3 to 4 minutes for dry), drain, then cool immediately in the ice bath. Once cooled, drain well, and add the noodles to the bowl with the toppings. Each diner can choose their own toppings for their separate bowls.
5. Distribute the hot broth among the bowls.
6. Serve immediately.

Tokyo-Style Tsukemen
Prep Time: 15 minutes | Cook Time: 30 minutes | Serves 4

- 18 ounces Basic Ramen Noodles (or store-bought) or 12 ounces dried ramen noodles
- 2 tablespoons neutral-flavored vegetable oil, divided
- 2 garlic cloves, minced
- 2 tablespoons chopped fresh ginger
- 2 shallots, minced
- 8 cups Tonkotsu
- ½ cup Shoyu Tare
- 12 slices Chashu Pork Belly
- ¼ cup sliced scallions, green and white parts
- 2 tablespoons sesame seeds
- 4 ounces enoki mushrooms
- 2 Soft-Boiled Eggs, halved lengthwise

1. Cook the noodles according to the recipe (or package instructions), drain, and rinse them under cold water, shaking the colander, to cool the noodles down.
2. In a large saucepan, heat 1 tablespoon of the oil over medium-high heat until it shimmers. Add the garlic, ginger, and shallots and cook, stirring frequently, until the shallot softens, about 5 minutes. Add the Tonkotsu and bring just to a boil. Reduce the heat and stir in the Shoyu Tare. Simmer, uncovered, for about 20 minutes, letting the broth reduce.
3. Meanwhile, heat the remaining tablespoon of vegetable oil in a skillet and warm the pork slices in it for 1 to 2 minutes on each side.
4. Divide the broth into 4 bowls and top with the scallions and sesame seeds, dividing equally.
5. Divide the noodles into 4 more separate bowls and top each with 3 slices of the pork, ¼ of the mushrooms, and half of 1 Soft-Boiled Egg. Serve immediately. Each diner gets a bowl of broth and a bowl of noodles, and should use the broth as a dipping sauce.

Pork Ramen with Kimchi, Fried Eggs, and Spam
Prep Time: 10 minutes | Cook Time: 10 minutes | Serves 4

- 4 (½-inch-thick) slices of Spam
- 4 large eggs
- 8 cups Basic Pork Broth or store-bought broth
- ½ cup Basic Shoyu Tare
- 18 ounces fresh ramen noodles, 12 ounces dried ramen noodles, or 2 packages instant ramen noodles, cooked according to package directions
- ½ cup kimchi

1. Heat a medium skillet over high heat. Put in the Spam and cook for 3 minutes, until browned on the bottom. Flip over and cook for 3 minutes more, until the second side is browned. Transfer the Spam to a plate.
2. In the same skillet, fry the eggs over medium heat, sunny-side up, until the whites are fully set and the yolks are still a bit runny, about 5 minutes.
3. In a pot, heat the broth over medium-high heat until simmering.
4. Into each of 4 serving bowls, put 2 tablespoons of tare. Divide the noodles among the bowls and ladle the broth over the noodles. Top each bowl with 1 slice of spam and 1 egg. Divide the kimchi among the bowls. Serve immediately.

Salt-Broiled Salmon Ramen with Corn and Greens
Prep Time: 10 minutes | Cook Time: 20 minutes | Serves 4

- 4 (4- to 6-ounce) salmon fillets, patted dry
- 1 teaspoon kosher salt
- 1 tablespoon cooking oil
- 10 chard or kale leaves, tough center ribs removed, leaves julienned
- 1½ cups fresh or frozen corn kernels
- 8 cups Basic Fish Broth
- ½ cup Basic Shoyu Tare
- 18 ounces fresh ramen noodles, 12 ounces dried ramen noodles, or 2 packages instant ramen noodles, cooked according to package directions
- 4 teaspoons Sesame-Chili Oil or store-bought sesame oil or chili oil

1. Preheat the broiler to high.
2. Season the salmon fillets on both sides with the salt and put them on a baking sheet.
3. Broil the salmon for 8 minutes, until it is cooked through and flakes easily with a fork.
4. In a medium skillet, heat the oil over medium-high heat. Add the greens and cook for 4 minutes, stirring, until wilted. Transfer them to a bowl.
5. Add the corn to the skillet and cook for 3 minutes, stirring, just until heated through and beginning to brown.
6. In a pot, heat the broth over medium-high heat until simmering.
7. Into each of 4 serving bowls, put 2 tablespoons of tare. Divide the noodles among the bowls and ladle the broth over the noodles. Top each bowl with a salmon fillet and divide the greens among the bowls. Drizzle each bowl with 1 teaspoon of sesame-chili oil. Serve immediately.

Tantanmen with Spicy Sesame Pork
Prep Time: 10 minutes | Cook Time: 10 minutes | Serves 4

- 1 pound ground pork
- 2 garlic cloves, minced
- 2 tablespoons peeled, minced fresh ginger
- 4 scallions, both white and green parts, thinly sliced and separated
- 2 tablespoons doubanjiang (fermented chile-bean paste)
- 1 tablespoon Japanese or Chinese sesame paste
- ½ teaspoon Szechuan peppercorns
- 8 cups Basic Pork Broth or store-bought broth
- ½ cup Spicy Miso Tare
- 18 ounces fresh ramen noodles, 12 ounces dried ramen noodles, or 2 packages instant ramen noodles, cooked according to package directions
- 4 teaspoons Sesame-Chili Oil or store-bought chili oil

1. In a large skillet, cook the pork over medium-high heat for about 5 minutes, stirring frequently, until the meat is browned. Add the garlic, ginger, and white parts of the scallions, and cook for 1 minute more. Stir in the doubanjiang, sesame paste, and Szechuan peppercorns, and cook for 1 minute more. Remove the skillet from the heat.
2. In a pot, heat the broth over medium-high heat until simmering.
3. Into each of 4 serving bowls, put 2 tablespoons of tare. Divide the noodles among the bowls and ladle the broth over the noodles. Top each bowl with the pork, scallion greens, and chili oil. Serve immediately.

Vegetarian Curry Ramen with Carrots, Peas, and Soft-Boiled Eggs
Prep Time: 15 minutes | Cook Time: 20 minutes | Serves 4

- 2 garlic cloves, peeled
- 1 (2-inch) piece peeled fresh ginger
- 1 shallot
- 1 tablespoon brown sugar
- 1 tablespoon curry powder
- 1 teaspoon ground coriander
- ½ teaspoon ground turmeric
- 1 tablespoon chili garlic paste
- ¼ teaspoon kosher salt
- 2 tablespoons neutral-flavored vegetable oil, divided
- 8 cups Shiitake Dashi
- 1 tablespoon soy sauce
- 2 carrots, diced
- 1 cup fresh or frozen peas
- 18 ounces Basic Ramen Noodles (or store-bought) or 12 ounces dried ramen noodles
- 2 Soft-Boiled Eggs, halved lengthwise
- 1 sheet nori, cut into 3-inch strips
- 4 radishes, thinly sliced
- ¼ cup chopped fresh cilantro

1. In a food processor, combine the garlic, ginger, shallot, brown sugar, curry powder, coriander, turmeric, chili garlic paste, and salt and process to a smooth purée.
2. In a large saucepan, heat 1 tablespoon of the oil over medium-high heat until it shimmers. Add the curry mixture and cook, stirring, for 1 minute. Add the Shiitake Dashi and reduce the heat to medium. Bring almost to a boil, then stir in the soy sauce.
3. In a small skillet, heat the remaining tablespoon of oil over medium-high heat until it shimmers. Add the carrots and cook, stirring frequently, until softened, about 5 minutes. Add the peas and cook, stirring, until just heated through, about 2 minutes more. Remove the pan from the heat.
4. Cook the noodles according to the recipe (or package instructions) and then drain well.
5. When the noodles are finished cooking, immediately ladle the hot broth into the serving bowls. Add ¼ of the noodles to each bowl and then lift the noodles up with chopsticks and gently lay them back into the broth, letting them float on top somewhat. Top each bowl with half of 1 Soft-Boiled Egg, ¼ of the peas and carrots mixture, ¼ of the nori strips, ¼ of the radishes, and 1 tablespoon of the cilantro. Serve immediately.

Thai-Style Green Curry Ramen with Grilled Steak, Squash, and Greens
Prep Time: 15 minutes | Cook Time: 20 minutes | Serves 4

- 2 tablespoons neutral-flavored vegetable oil
- 2 garlic cloves, minced
- 1 tablespoon minced fresh ginger
- 1 to 3 tablespoons Thai green curry paste
- 1 tablespoon brown sugar
- 6½ cups Clear Chicken Broth
- 4 cups fresh spinach
- 1 (15-ounce) can coconut milk
- 1 tablespoon fish sauce
- 1 pound top sirloin steak, about ½-inch thick
- Kosher salt
- Freshly ground black pepper
- 2 cups diced kabocha squash
- 18 ounces Basic Ramen Noodles (or store-bought) or 12 ounces dried ramen noodles
- ¼ cup chopped fresh cilantro
- 1 lime, cut into wedges, for garnish

1. In a stockpot, heat the oil over medium heat. Add the garlic, ginger, and Thai green curry paste and cook, stirring, for 2 minutes. Add the brown sugar and cook, stirring, for 1 minute more. Add the Clear Chicken Broth and raise the heat to medium-high. Bring almost to a boil. Add the spinach and cook for 1 to 2 minutes, until just wilted. Use a slotted spoon to remove the spinach from the broth.
2. Stir the coconut milk and fish sauce into the broth and heat until it comes back up to almost boiling.
3. Preheat the grill to medium-high heat. Season the steak generously with salt and pepper and grill for about 3 minutes per side for medium-rare. Remove from the heat and let rest for at least 5 minutes before slicing against the grain into ¼-inch-thick slices.
4. Place the squash in a medium microwave-safe bowl and add ⅓ cup water. Cover and heat in the microwave for 3 to 5 minutes, until the squash is tender. Drain.
5. Cook the noodles according to the recipe (or package instructions) and then drain well.
6. When the noodles are finished cooking, immediately ladle the hot broth into the serving bowls. Add ¼ of the noodles to each bowl and then lift the noodles up with chopsticks and gently lay them back into the broth, letting them float on top somewhat.
7. Top each bowl with ¼ of the steak, ¼ of the squash, ¼ of the spinach, and 1 tablespoon of the cilantro. Serve immediately with a wedge of lime for diners to squeeze into the soup as desired.

Vegan Chili Tofu Ramen
Prep Time: 10 minutes | Cook Time: 50 minutes | Serves 4

- 1 lb dried shiitake mushrooms
- 1 tablespoon sake
- 1 tablespoon mirin
- 2 tablespoons soy sauce
- 1 garlic clove, bashed
- 1 thumb-sized ginger piece, chopped
- 2 red chilies, 1 sliced in half, 1 finely sliced
- 8 cups water
- 2 cups kale or spinach, shredded
- 2 handfuls bean sprouts
- 4 servings egg-free ramen noodles
- 160g pack marinated tofu, cut into pieces
- chili or garlic oil, to taste
- 2 spring onions, finely sliced

1. Add mushrooms, sake, mirin, soy sauce, garlic, ginger, and halved chili in a large pan and cover with 8 cups of water. Simmer for 30 minutes, until mushrooms are tender and stock becomes fragrant.
2. Strain prepared stock into a clean pot and bring to a gentle simmer again. Remove mushrooms and slice them, discard chili, ginger and garlic. Blanch bean sprouts and drain them well.
3. Cook noodles in boiling water, drain and divide among 4 soup bowls. Add mushrooms, greens, bean sprouts and tofu to the stock to warm them for 3-4 minutes.
4. Divide tofu and vegetables among the bowls evenly, and pour over the vegetable stock.
5. Top with a few dots of chili oil, and sprinkle with spring onions.

Appendix 1 Measurement Conversion Chart

Volume Equivalents (Dry)	
US STANDARD	METRIC (APPROXIMATE)
1/8 teaspoon	0.5 mL
1/4 teaspoon	1 mL
1/2 teaspoon	2 mL
3/4 teaspoon	4 mL
1 teaspoon	5 mL
1 tablespoon	15 mL
1/4 cup	59 mL
1/2 cup	118 mL
3/4 cup	177 mL
1 cup	235 mL
2 cups	475 mL
3 cups	700 mL
4 cups	1 L

Volume Equivalents (Liquid)		
US STANDARD	US STANDARD (OUNCES)	METRIC (APPROXIMATE)
2 tablespoons	1 fl.oz.	30 mL
1/4 cup	2 fl.oz.	60 mL
1/2 cup	4 fl.oz.	120 mL
1 cup	8 fl.oz.	240 mL
1 1/2 cup	12 fl.oz.	355 mL
2 cups or 1 pint	16 fl.oz.	475 mL
4 cups or 1 quart	32 fl.oz.	1 L
1 gallon	128 fl.oz.	4 L

Temperatures Equivalents	
FAHRENHEIT(F)	CELSIUS(C) APPROXIMATE)
225 °F	107 °C
250 °F	120 ° °C
275 °F	135 °C
300 °F	150 °C
325 °F	160 °C
350 °F	180 °C
375 °F	190 °C
400 °F	205 °C
425 °F	220 °C
450 °F	235 °C
475 °F	245 °C
500 °F	260 °C

Weight Equivalents	
US STANDARD	METRIC (APPROXIMATE)
1 ounce	28 g
2 ounces	57 g
5 ounces	142 g
10 ounces	284 g
15 ounces	425 g
16 ounces (1 pound)	455 g
1.5 pounds	680 g
2 pounds	907 g

Appendix 2 The Dirty Dozen and Clean Fifteen

The Environmental Working Group (EWG) is a nonprofit, nonpartisan organization dedicated to protecting human health and the environment Its mission is to empower people to live healthier lives in a healthier environment. This organization publishes an annual list of the twelve kinds of produce, in sequence, that have the highest amount of pesticide residue-the Dirty Dozen-as well as a list of the fifteen kinds of produce that have the least amount of pesticide residue-the Clean Fifteen.

THE DIRTY DOZEN	
The 2016 Dirty Dozen includes the following produce. These are considered among the year's most important produce to buy organic:	
Strawberries	Spinach
Apples	Tomatoes
Nectarines	Bell peppers
Peaches	Cherry tomatoes
Celery	Cucumbers
Grapes	Kale/collard greens
Cherries	Hot peppers
The Dirty Dozen list contains two additional itemskale/collard greens and hot peppers-because they tend to contain trace levels of highly hazardous pesticides.	

THE CLEAN FIFTEEN	
The least critical to buy organically are the Clean Fifteen list. The following are on the 2016 list:	
Avocados	Papayas
Corn	Kiw
Pineapples	Eggplant
Cabbage	Honeydew
Sweet peas	Grapefruit
Onions	Cantaloupe
Asparagus	Cauliflower
Mangos	
Some of the sweet corn sold in the United States are made from genetically engineered (GE) seedstock. Buy organic varieties of these crops to avoid GE produce.	

Appendix 3 Index

A

all-purpose flour 50, 53
allspice 15
almond 5, 14
ancho chile 10
ancho chile powder 5
apple 9
apple cider vinegar 9
arugula 51
avocado 11

B

bacon 52
balsamic vinegar 7, 12, 52
basil 5, 8, 11, 13
beet 52
bell pepper 50, 51, 53
black beans 50, 51
broccoli 51, 52, 53
buns 52
butter 50

C

canola oil 50, 51, 52
carrot 52, 53
cauliflower 5, 52
cayenne 5, 52
cayenne pepper 52
Cheddar cheese 52
chicken 6
chili powder 50, 51
chipanle pepper 50
chives 5, 6, 52
cinnamon 15
coconut 6
Colby Jack cheese 51
coriander 52
corn 50, 51
corn kernels 50
cumin 5, 10, 15, 50, 51, 52

D

diced panatoes 50
Dijon mustard 7, 12, 13, 51
dry onion powder 52

E

egg 14, 50, 53
enchilada sauce 51

F

fennel seed 53
flour 50, 53
fresh chives 5, 6, 52
fresh cilantro 52
fresh cilantro leaves 52
fresh dill 5
fresh parsley 6, 52
fresh parsley leaves 52

G

garlic 5, 9, 10, 11, 13, 14, 50, 51, 52, 53
garlic powder 8, 9, 52, 53

H

half-and-half 50
hemp seeds 8
honey 9, 51

I

instant rice 51

K

kale 14
kale leaves 14
ketchup 53
kosher salt 5, 10, 15

L

lemon 5, 6, 14, 51, 53
lemon juice 6, 8, 11, 13, 14, 51
lime 9, 12
lime juice 9, 12
lime zest 9, 12

M

maple syrup 7, 12, 53
Marinara Sauce 5
micro greens 52
milk 5, 50
mixed berries 12
Mozzarella 50, 53
Mozzarella cheese 50, 53
mushroom 51, 52
mustard 51, 53
mustard powder 53

64 | Ramen For Beginners

N

nutritional yeast 5

O

olive oil 5, 12, 13, 14, 50, 51, 52, 53
onion 5, 50, 51
onion powder 8
oregano 5, 8, 10, 50

P

panatoes 50, 52
paprika 5, 15, 52
Parmesan cheese 51, 53
parsley 6, 52
pesto 52
pink Himalayan salt 5, 7, 8, 11
pizza dough 50, 53
pizza sauce 50
plain coconut yogurt 6
plain Greek yogurt 5
porcini powder 53
potato 53

R

Ranch dressing 52
raw honey 9, 12, 13
red pepper flakes 5, 8, 14, 15, 51, 53
ricotta cheese 53

S

saffron 52
Serrano pepper 53
sugar 10
summer squash 51

T

tahini 5, 8, 9, 11
thyme 50
toasted almonds 14
tomato 5, 50, 52, 53
turmeric 15

U

unsalted butter 50
unsweetened almond milk 5

V

vegetable broth 50
vegetable stock 51

W

white wine 8, 11
wine vinegar 8, 10, 11

Y

yogurt 5, 6

Z

zucchini 50, 51, 52, 53

SAYA TSUDA